Jamie
KENNEDY
Kitchens

J.K.

J.K.

THE JAMIE KENNEDY COOKBOOK

Jamie Kennedy with Ivy Knight

Photography by Jo Dickins

HarperCollins*Publishers*Ltd

HarperCollins Publishers Ltd
2 Bloor Street East, 20th Floor
Toronto, Ontario, Canada
M4W 1A8

www.harpercollins.ca

Library and Archives Canada Cataloguing in
Publication information is available upon request.

ISBN 978-1-44341-900-0

Printed and bound in Canada

9 8 7 6 5 4 3 2 1

To my mother and father, Patricia and John.
To my children, Julia, Micha, Jackson and Nile.
To my darling Victoria.

Contents

Foreword

I met Jamie Kennedy for the first time in 1977 in Lucerne, Switzerland, where we worked at the Grand Hotel National. From that day we became good friends, sharing parallel interests in cooking, music and culture. As chefs de cuisine at what is now a Toronto dining institution, Scaramouche, we started the movement of local Ontario cuisine, which involved looking for that farmer or gardener who had that ripe, tasty, in-season and, most of the time, organic product. That's what we were looking for! I think this is what Ontario's farmers' markets are all about today. Jamie has never wavered in his support and use of local Ontario products. In 1989 we founded Knives & Forks and created Feast of Fields in Ontario, which has since grown to become an annual nationwide event.

Jamie's resilient spirit has carried him through the ups and downs of the restaurant industry, and he continues to be a pillar of integrity and inspiration. This book is not just about his cooking, recipes and love for food. It's also about Jamie telling you his stories and about the milestone experiences of his life. It's a wonderful history of how we got to where we are now in the culinary world, told through Jamie's eyes.

Much of the food we enjoy in Canadian restaurants today is a result of Jamie's work in the local food movement, as he has influenced generations of chefs who share his pioneering spirit and love for real food.

Jamie's appreciation of classical French cuisine and his knowledge of Canadian food culture are essential ingredients of this book. In this way, Jamie's book is a celebration of all things Canadian, most particularly how living in Canada allows us to learn about the many cultures that influence our national palate.

—Michael Stadtländer, Chef and co-owner of Eigensinn Farm and Haisai

Introductions

I pause to take stock. I review the passage of time since I last published a cookbook, in 2000. I am riding a new wave in my career that reflects a collective evolution in gastronomy for Southern Ontario. As a culture interested in food, we have grown past our infancy. In the past we learned by imitating other food cultures more advanced than ours. Now we have reached the point of leaving the house, not to travel abroad but rather to stay in the neighbourhood to explore and absorb excellence right here at home. In the last few years we have witnessed a proliferation of farmers' markets. It is possible in Toronto to visit a different farmers' market each day of the week, and that speaks to where we are heading in our new consciousness, how we view the food and wine that winds up on our table. It is a delicious evolution. The foods, the wines and the people of Ontario form an identity that is unique to this place. We belong together, around the table and in the community we inhabit.

As I travel around North America, I observe a similar phenomenon wherever I visit. What is common is the pride of place and the pride in the people involved in transforming local raw ingredients into delicious food on the plate and wine in the glass; these carry with them a harmony that resonates with a unique cultural experience wherever it is practised.

Speaking of community, it has been wonderful to collaborate with my co-authors, Jo and Ivy, to create this book. At earlier times in my career, I felt it was important to isolate myself in order to tap into my creativity. To some degree it is still important for me to do that, but now I feel much better about letting others in on the creative and operational challenges of the enterprise. My new approach to the creative process is also symbolic of the new wave in food culture. My creative process is more informed by the people around me than ever before. There is more sharing in the struggles and successes of the enterprise, and this leads to a greater sense of shared accomplishment. This collaborative approach has a wonderful flow about it that allows the team to cover more ground.

The recipes in this book vary in degree of difficulty. Many stem from my experience working in professional kitchens. In my kitchen, everything is prepared from scratch and with a deep respect for the ingredients and process involved in achieving excellence. The recipes can seem difficult at times, but if you don't mind spending the time you will find among them some gems that will become part of your repertoire.

The book itself is really a collection of stories and ideas put together by someone who has witnessed a culture come of age, from the point of view of an active participant, spanning four decades of engagement.

—JAMIE KENNEDY

It all started at a casual lunch at the Drake Hotel with my friend Rob Firing, the head of publicity for HarperCollins Canada. We were talking about different chefs we admired when Jamie Kennedy's name came up. "I wish he'd do a cookbook with us," Rob sighed. Then he looked at me, a twinkle in his eye: "Why don't you convince him to do a book with you as the author?"

I leapt at the opportunity. For the past seven years, I had been writing about food and Toronto's culinary scene for newspapers and magazines in Canada and the United States, but I'd never written a book. I emailed Jamie right away and asked to meet. He had ten minutes free the following week, so I booked it, we met and I gave him the pitch.

"No way." He'd already done two books and knew how much work they were; he was too busy. It just wasn't possible.

I was not going to lose this opportunity just because the linchpin wasn't interested. I pressed on. "When you wrote the other two books," I told him, "you did all the work yourself. This book will be different. There will be a team creating the book, with you as the leader." Joanna Dickins, Jamie's assistant and his photographer, would do the photos and help us arrange the layout. I would do all the writing. Jamie would just have to compile the recipes. I put it to him another way: "You would be the head chef; Jo and I would be your sous-chefs."

He smiled—that seemed to click with him. He agreed, and the work began. We came up with ideas for topics to cover, topics important to Jamie and his career—French fries, apprenticeship, scrambled eggs. Then I would set up my iPhone, press Record and ask Jamie to tell me his thoughts on Ontario cheese or ask him how he ended up planting a vineyard on his farm. His eloquence and vast knowledge are all here in these pages.

My intention throughout this whole process was to keep at bay the earnestness that so often pervades the words of any chef who sources his ingredients with care. Jamie was one of the first chefs in this country to let local ingredients dictate his menu and to introduce Ontario producers to his devoted customers, but that doesn't mean he spends his days writing love letters to farmers and fondling heirloom beets. Jamie is a chef who has worked incredibly hard in this business for over forty years—in fact, while other chefs his age spend most of their day giving interviews and Instagramming selfies, you can still find Jamie on the line at Gilead leading his team through service. He doesn't crave celebrity, he works as hard as anyone on his crew and he does the best impression of Stadtländer I've ever heard.

I've included in the book a number of quotes from the friends, fans, cooks and customers he has influenced and inspired over the years. Most cookbooks are written in one voice, that of the chef, but for this one we wanted to give you a chance to understand Jamie from as many viewpoints as possible, including mine and Jo's.

While putting together this book, I got to see past the living legend into what kind of a man Jamie is. He is a hippy with a very loving way of looking at the world. His calm demeanour and easy smile put anyone within his radius at ease. Unlike other chefs, there is no burning rage or jittery egomania in him. He is a tradesman with the soul of a painter and a very big heart.

—IVY KNIGHT

I met Jamie Kennedy because of Arlene Stein, a champion of the Toronto culinary scene and the founder of the Terroir Symposium. (I'm sure she's responsible for many a life-changing introduction.) She asked me to photograph her first Terroir Symposium in 2007, where Jamie was the keynote speaker. Later, Arlene and I embarked on a book project together, in the course of which we went on a day trip to Prince Edward County, where we toured Jamie's farm. After a few more chance meetings, I told Jamie that I wanted to do a book just about him. Jamie and I got to know each other, playing some tennis and discussing Slow Food, music and other creative topics. By 2008 I was photographing him in action at events; one thing led to another and I became his official photographer. Soon after, I joined his team as his assistant. This became rather an overwhelming but interesting role, but between that and the constant craziness that is the life of a chef, my book idea with Jamie took a back seat.

Enter Ivy Knight . . . Ivy was what we needed to bring the project back to the front burner and to make it a reality.

Jamie has been my muse for the last several years, and I'm grateful for the opportunity to be witness to his world. Through my photographs I hope to share my observations and impressions of him, and his culture and philosophies, in action.

—JO DICKINS

A Note about Ingredients

Unless otherwise specified, I use these ingredients in my recipes:

salt: fine sea salt
oil: non-genetically-modified (non-GMO) sunflower oil
eggs: organic, free-run large eggs
milk: 2%
butter: unsalted

A Note about Food Photography

Many of the food photographs in this book were captured *in situ* during service and as such they were not styled specifically to match each recipe. However, I try to give suggestions for achieving the restaurant garnishes in most cases.

early days

JAMIE KENNEDY WAS FASCINATED

BY THE THEATRE OF RESTAURANTS

AND FELL IN LOVE WITH COOKING AS IT

WAS BROUGHT TO LIFE BY JULIA CHILD ON TV.

From High School to Head Chef

In high school, at Loomis Chaffee in Connecticut, I was the president of the cooking club. I watched Julia Child and *The Galloping Gourmet* on TV, so I thought I knew something about cooking. I was seventeen. I had grown up in Toronto, but there were about six years when my family lived in the U.S. My dad was teaching video arts at Yale, giving me an opportunity to go to boarding school nearby. Everyone at Loomis was in a club—Golf, Stamps, Russian, Jazz—so I started the Culinary Club.

There was a girl who I had a crush on, a day student, and I asked her if she wanted to be a co-president of this Culinary Club. We needed a venue off campus to host dinner parties, so she got permission from her parents and volunteered her house. We had a faculty chaperone who allowed us to buy wine to drink with our dinners. I had argued to faculty that if we were going to discover the dishes of Burgundy, then we also needed to drink the wines of Burgundy, and they said okay. Crazy! As long as there was a chaperone it was fine. We'd pick a region, then go to the library and research it and plan a menu. We did Burgundy, Italy, Mexico and Russia. I think about that now—the school letting a bunch of high school students drink! But those were more liberal times, the late '60s, early '70s.

I graduated at seventeen. That same year, my family moved back to Toronto. I felt like I needed to take some time away from school and work as an apprentice cook. In three years I'd be twenty, and if I still felt like going to university I could, but I'd also have a skill behind me so I could help pay for my education while at school. My parents Geoff gave me their blessing, and I have never looked back.

After five years in the industry I was offered the job of chef at Scaramouche restaurant. It's kind of a crazy progression to have that kind of opportunity only five years into your career. When the offer came in, I was working as a commis in the Grand Hotel National in Lucerne, Switzerland. It was while working at this hotel that I met Michael Stadtländer. We became friends, and he was always asking about what it was like in Canada. He really wanted to come here. I talked to Michael about the offer that I had just received to be head chef at this Toronto restaurant-to-be. I became more excited about accepting the offer when Michael and I decided we would do it together.

I talked to some of my chef mentors who had trained me. People weren't opening restaurants li
in Toronto at that time. There were Chinese restaurants or steakhouses or chains, but there weren
many stand-alone restaurants doing interesting things. My chefs thought I needed to spend much
time in the field. This was an era where the chefs holding positions of power in the city were all expat Sw
German, French, Italians. They brought their old-school values to bear when thinking about a young co
being offered a job as head chef. Of course they were opposed to the idea. I went ahead anyway.

Certainly it was an incredible opportunity and a huge challenge for a couple of twenty-three-year-olds—
all of a sudden being the boss of fifteen people, reporting to owners, having to have a rapport with the publi
being written up by the critics. It was a wild time. In some ways I do regret the decision, because I was having
a pretty nice time as a transient young cook working in Europe, having a blast working in seasonal hotels.
There were always really cool people, great activities and wonderful opportunities. When you're actually
living and working in a place, you become kind of a citizen. It's different from the tourist experience. I was
enjoying that.

Scaramouche yanked me out of that world. The part I regret is that I took on all that responsibility as a
young kid. The part that was amazing was that I took on all that responsibility as a young kid. It's certainly
served me well.

10

I remember hearing that Morden Yolles, the owner of Scaramouche, had discovered Jamie in Switzerland and hired him to be the chef. It was predicted that Jamie was going to be very "big" and that Scaramouche was going to be one of the best restaurants in Toronto.

I think I remember that moment because it was so exciting. Toronto was a different place then— food was just beginning to play an important role in people's lives, the restaurant industry was just starting to emerge as a force, but becoming a chef was still regarded as an alternative career. It was exciting to hear of a bright, young chef and exciting that a fantastic new restaurant was about to open. It was a look into the future.

BONNIE STERN, FOOD WRITER AND COOKBOOK AUTHOR

The Swiss Butcher's Apprentice

When some apprentices come into this industry, they have a romantic view of cooking. Those initial passionate feelings are ones that should be preserved in spite of what follows, because what follows brings you crashing down to earth. That's when you decide if you really want to be a cook. It's not an easy life, and moments of glory come few and far between. They happen, but only as punctuation to a lot of drudgery. Preserving the optimism as a hedge against the cynicism setting in is a good idea.

I got my first job as an apprentice at the Windsor Arms Hotel in Toronto. My chef there asked me, "Why do you want to become a cook?" And this exuberant seventeen-year-old responded, "Because I love cooking!" He was probably the same age I am now, he had huge bags under his eyes, the ashtray on his desk was overflowing with cigarette butts, and he just started laughing this huge laugh. But then he hired me.

I was thrown onto the restaurant line. I'd show up at two thirty and get ready for service. I didn't have a specific position, I just did whatever they needed me to do. The restaurant was called Three Small Rooms. One room was the wine cellar, where you walked down into this cozy candlelit room and they'd present fondue in these Le Creuset pots, so I mastered fondue. I could make cheese fondue! I was on top of the world. I did other things too, like gratinéing whole Dover soles with some kind of compound butter.

I did that for about two months, until the Swiss sous-chef, Ulrich Herzig, who ran the kitchen during the day, decided he wanted an apprentice. He approached the chef and asked if he could take me on days and teach me the basics, but the chef wanted to keep me on the line. They got into a huge fight. Herzig's point was that you don't take a young kid who knows nothing about cooking and put him on the line, where he's just dealing with finished product, working with things that he has no idea how to make. He won the argument and I started working days with him, and that's when my apprenticeship really began.

Herzig was a master butcher. He was also a master garde manger. We were making terrines and pâtés, galantines and pâtés en croute. We had to make all these things as well as basic sauces and stocks for the hotel. One of the first things Herzig let me do in the butchery department was chicken. Chicken, chicken, chicken, broken down, boned out. For the restaurant they had to be suprêmed, for the café it was whole chickens cut up, then for the galantine of capon the bird was completely boned out. Six months with chicken

13

and then I moved on to lamb racks, then lamb legs, then veal legs. All this time doing all the stocks and demi-glace. I worked with Herzig for two and a half years. From eight in the morning until ten thirty, I'd clean all the fridges, replace all the ice on the fish and set up his station. Then I went into Three Small Rooms to set up the grill and garde-manger for lunch service. I'd do grill orders and garde-manger orders for all three rooms. At two thirty I'd clean my stations and then go back and work for Herzig until the day ended.

My own apprenticeship experience informs how I approach teaching the elements of cooking to my apprentices here at Jamie Kennedy Kitchens.

When I started my apprenticeship I was passionate and worked my butt off, but I wasn't any good. Jamie puts his apprentices through four or five months on a station. Jamie and his head production chef, Ken Steele, take you through everything you need to know to be successful on every station. It is structured so you don't do things too fast. They don't ever swear at you or yell at you, but they still push you to get better or try harder. If Jamie's production chefs were busy, Jamie would step in and show you his steps. He talks with his hands a lot and makes it easy to learn. He's almost like a hippy in the way he deals with people, he's so chill and relaxed, and that makes his kitchen such a good learning environment.

I've been blessed—not many cooks get to have the experiences I've had in the short time I've been cooking. If I didn't have Jamie as my mentor, none of that would have happened. When I first started working with him he showed me a potato and he started telling me how beautiful the potato was and I thought he was nuts, I thought, "This guy is loony-tunes." But now I get it.

NICK WALTERS, FORMER APPRENTICE, J.K. ALUMNI

French Onion Soup

Makes 6 servings

For the first month or so that I worked at the Windsor Arms Hotel, I had no idea what was going on. It was a busy place, with waiters rushing in and out and the cooks swearing at the waiters for bringing them orders. At first I was shocked by the language, but then I realized that this was one way of dealing with the hot, stressful environment. I was assigned to be a small cog in the wheel in a hot, stressful environment of my own. There was a giant broiler called a salamander, with an oven mounted on top of it that got incredibly scorching. The heat emanating from this apparatus quickly incinerated all the hair on my fingers and forearms; it only grew back years later when I went on vacation and got a break from the kitchen.

French onion soup was on the menu, and I was responsible for preparing this dish when it was ordered. A ladle of soup always warm from the bain-marie went into a special handled crock. Then a couple of slices of house-made melba toast. Then a generous sprinkling of grated Gruyère cheese. Under the salamander for a moment and hey presto, a golden, bubbling, gooey bowl of delicious comfort food.

Here in Southern Ontario, a semi-soft melting cheese such as Niagara Gold or Thunder Oak Gouda works admirably in place of Gruyère.

Ingredients

3 medium onions, thinly sliced

4 tablespoons (60 g) butter

1 cup (250 mL) dry red wine

12 cups (3 L) beef stock

2 bay leaves

2 whole cloves

Salt and freshly ground black pepper

12 slices melba toast or lightly toasted
   baguette slices

4 ounces (125 g) Gruyère, grated

Directions

In a large soup pot, gently sauté the onions in the butter over medium-low heat, stirring frequently, until the onions are evenly golden brown, about 30 minutes.

Pour in the red wine and cook, stirring and scraping up the brown bits on the bottom of the pan, until the wine has reduced by about half. Add the beef stock, bay leaves and cloves and simmer for an additional 45 minutes. Season with salt and pepper. Discard the bay leaves.

Preheat the broiler. Lay out 6 onion soup bowls on a baking sheet. Ladle hot soup into each bowl. Place 2 slices of crisp toasts on top of each serving. Sprinkle generously with grated cheese. Broil until the cheese is bubbly and golden brown. Serve.

Whitefish Quenelles

Makes 6 servings

This is another dish that hails from the French canon. This one comes from Burgundy. There, the fish used is primarily pike, and the sauce is made with crayfish from the same waters as the pike. I have adapted the recipe to make use of our Ontario whitefish, although you can still use pike if you have it. I don't use crayfish in the beurre blanc, preferring to add a hint of anise flavour with fresh tarragon instead. At the restaurant I serve these with seasonal vegetables.

Ingredients

Quenelles

Approximately 1 pound (500 g) fresh skinless whitefish fillets, cut into small pieces

6 ice cubes

6 tablespoons (100 g) butter, softened

1 clove garlic, finely minced

1 teaspoon (5 mL) pastis or other anise liqueur

A squeeze of fresh lemon juice

Salt and freshly ground black pepper

7 tablespoons (100 mL) whipping cream

3 egg yolks

Beurre Blanc

2 cups (500 mL) dry white wine

7 tablespoons (100 mL) white wine vinegar

1 teaspoon (5 mL) tarragon vinegar

2 bay leaves

6 black peppercorns, coarsely ground

2 or 3 sprigs of fresh tarragon

3 shallots, thinly sliced

6 tablespoons (100 g) cold butter, cut into small cubes

1 teaspoon (5 mL) chopped fresh tarragon

Directions

To make the quenelle mixture, place about one-third of the cut-up whitefish and a couple of ice cubes in your food processor; process until smooth. While the processor is running, add one-third each of the softened butter, garlic and pastis. Add lemon juice, salt and pepper to taste. Add one-third of the cream in a slow, steady stream. Add 1 egg yolk. Continue processing until smooth and well combined.

Stop the machine. Using a spatula, scrape down the sides and bottom of the bowl. Run the machine for a few more seconds to ensure a homogenous consistency. Scrape the mixture into a medium bowl. Repeat the process two more times, combining the quenelle mixture. Reserve.

recipe continues . . .

To make the beurre blanc, in a small nonreactive saucepan, combine the white wine, white wine vinegar, tarragon vinegar, bay leaves, ground peppercorns, tarragon sprigs and shallots. Bring to the boil, then reduce heat and simmer slowly until the mixture is syrupy and almost dry. Remove from the heat and whisk in the cold butter all at once until completely melted and the sauce is emulsified, returning the pot to the element briefly to help melt the butter. Discard the bay leaves. Stir in the chopped tarragon.

Transfer the beurre blanc to a blender and purée. Pour the sauce into a small pitcher and keep in a warm place while you poach the quenelles.

Fill a large, wide saucepan or sauté pan with salted water and bring to a simmer. When the water is simmering, use 2 soup spoons to form the quenelle mixture into 12 egg-shaped quenelles. Carefully place the quenelles in the water and gently poach for 5 minutes or until they bob to the surface and plump up.

Transfer the quenelles with a slotted spoon to paper towels and let them drain briefly. Divide them among 6 plates. Nap the quenelles with some of the beurre blanc. Serve.

Roast Galantine of Cornish Hen with Succotash

Makes 2 servings

I used to watch in awe as my chef at the Windsor Arms, Ulrich Herzig, would bone out capons, leaving them whole, cutting the skin only along the back, and laying them out flat on sheets of muslin coated with sliced pork back fat. Next he would prepare a forcemeat from the breast and leg trim and mix in pistachios and little cubes of back fat and ham. Then he would stuff the capons, wrap the whole issue back up in a shape resembling the bird before it had been boned, and tie them securely. While they poached gently, the capons filled the kitchen with rich, exotic aromas. We would serve chilled slices with a small salad and Cumberland sauce in the Courtyard Café.

This recipe is a variation on that one, and I've given it a Canadian infusion. It is served warm with the "three sisters" combination of squash, beans and corn from First Nations tradition. Ask your butcher to bone out your hen in a way that keeps all the skin on the breast and legs intact.

Ingredients

Galantine of Cornish Hen

1 large Cornish hen, boned, keeping breast and leg skin intact
1 clove garlic, finely minced
1 teaspoon (5 mL) finely chopped fresh rosemary
1 teaspoon (5 mL) finely chopped fresh summer savory
1 teaspoon (5 mL) finely chopped fresh sage
4 tablespoons (60 mL) sunflower oil
Salt and freshly ground black pepper

Succotash

1 medium onion, finely chopped
4 tablespoons (60 mL) sunflower oil
Kernels from 2 corn cobs
1 medium zucchini, diced
½ cup (125 mL) cooked dried lima or other beans
1 tablespoon (15 mL) roughly chopped fresh sage
Salt and freshly ground black pepper

Directions

Preheat the oven to 350°F (180°C).

To make the galantine, lay out the boned hen on a work surface, skin side down. Combine the garlic, rosemary, savory and sage with 2 tablespoons

(30 mL) of the sunflower oil. Smear this mixture over the flesh of the hen. Fold each leg over each breast, then fold the breasts together to make a package that has the breast in the centre and the legs on the outside. Truss with butcher's string.

Season the galantine with salt and pepper. Place in a small roasting pan. Pour the remaining 2 tablespoons (30 mL) sunflower oil over the galantine. Roast, basting from time to time, until a meat thermometer registers 150°F (65°C), approximately 40 minutes.

Meanwhile, prepare the succotash. In a frying pan over medium heat, gently sauté the onion in the sunflower oil, without colouring, for 5 minutes. Add the corn, zucchini and beans and gently sauté for an additional 10 minutes or until all the vegetables are tender. Remove from the heat; stir in the sage and season with salt and pepper. Reserve, keeping warm.

Remove the galantine from the oven and transfer to a cutting board. When cool enough to handle, remove the string.

Set out 2 dinner plates. Spoon succotash onto each plate. Place 2 carved slices of Cornish hen on each mound of succotash. Spoon a little of the pan juices over each slice of hen. Serve.

This old woodstove warms the "gallery," where Jamie hosts dinners on his farm.

spring

THE CREEKS OVERFLOW THEIR BANKS,

FORMING CONDUITS TO THE GREAT LAKES. IT'S A

TIME FOR RENEWAL AND OPTIMISM, AND

EXCITED ANTICIPATION FOR THE UPCOMING

GROWING SEASON.

Rhubarb Revelations

Rhubarb has such a great flavour, so complex, almost savoury. Even though we put in loads of sugar to make it palatable, I do think of it as something savoury, or at least something with a savoury depth. I grew up with kids whose grandmothers were from East Germany, and these women would eat rhubarb raw, just dipped in salt. I tried it once, but I didn't like it. If you eat it raw, what you're mainly processing is the tartness. It doesn't give you the depths of flavour that it does once sugar is added to it.

The leaves are poisonous. You'll notice that not too many insects attack it, so you don't have to spray it. It is such a generous plant that keeps giving all summer long.

I once visited St. Andrews by-the-Sea in New Brunswick to cook a dinner with Chef Chris Aerni. He and his wife, Graziella, own the Rossmount Inn. On the first day, Chris took me on a tour of the area so we could find ingredients that would inspire our menu. We went to a woman's farm—it was a very small farm but her gardens were beautiful. She had an apple tree where she had grafted different varieties of apples to the branches, so that one tree had eight different varieties growing on it. Her rhubarb was amazing—the stalks were long and deeply hued. I decided that I would make a rhubarb dessert for the dinner. I made a rhubarb jelly and the colour was just mind-bogglingly beautiful. It was pink but it was almost iridescent, with blue coming out of it too. Everyone was just blown away by the colour, it was psychedelic.

Rhubarb is unique. It should be used more often than it is. When you think about the first edibles that appear out of the ground in the spring, ramps and fiddleheads get all the glory. What about the rhubarb?

Rhubarb Jelly

Makes six 1-pint (500 mL) jars

Rhubarb is one of the first perennial plants to present itself each year. Although it is used in several northern and eastern European cultures, it is a crop that is also distinctly Canadian. I love it in many forms, but as a jelly to spread on toast in the morning or to garnish a cheese plate, it is unsurpassed.

Ingredients

11 pounds (5 kg) fresh field-grown rhubarb
1 cup (250 mL) water
5 pounds (2.5 kg) fine granulated sugar
½ cup (125 mL) liquid pectin

Directions

For canning instructions, see pages 282–83.

Cut rhubarb into small pieces and put it in a large nonreactive pot. Add the water. Bring to the boil, then reduce heat to a simmer and cover. Cook until the rhubarb is very soft, stirring from time to time, approximately 15 minutes.

Suspend a cheesecloth-lined colander over another large nonreactive pot. Transfer the rhubarb mixture to the colander and let drain overnight in the refrigerator.

Discard the rhubarb. Measure approximately 12 cups (3 L) of the rhubarb juice. Add the sugar to the rhubarb juice. Bring to the boil, stirring to dissolve the sugar, and boil vigorously for 10 minutes, skimming off the foam from time to time. Stir in the liquid pectin and boil for an additional 3 minutes.

Pour the jelly into 6 sterilized 1-pint (500 mL) mason jars, leaving ¼-inch (5 mm) headspace. Seal jars and process in boiling water for 15 minutes. Cool on the counter and store in a cool, dark place.

Rhubarb Jelly with Chocolate and Maple

Makes 6 servings

In 2010, I staged a big communal-table event at Evergreen Brick Works. Three hundred people sat together around a big table, dining on Ontario's bounty. But there was another sense of community I felt that day, in the way many of my friends in the restaurant industry rallied around me in an effort to raise money for my organization. I had experienced some hard times, and were it not for my community stepping in to lend a helping hand, I might have lost everything. When I look back at that time, I am amazed by how much my own crisis taught me about my business and my life in general. It forced me to turn over several leaves and recalibrate my approach. Ironically enough, I believe it has inspired my creativity and given me renewed passion for my work. We served this dessert at the communal table (see page 161), garnished with edible flowers.

Ingredients

Rhubarb Jelly

2 pounds (1 kg) fresh field-grown rhubarb
¾ cup (175 g) granulated sugar
2 tablespoons (30 mL) water
5 gelatin sheets, soaked in cold water to soften

Chocolate Ganache

3½ ounces (100 g) 70% dark chocolate,
    broken into small pieces
7 tablespoons (100 mL) whipping cream

Maple Cream

½ cup (125 mL) maple syrup
¼ cup (60 mL) whipping cream

Garnish

3 tablespoons (50 mL) fresh rhubarb cut into
    julienne, held in cold water so it curls
Fresh mint sprigs
Granulated maple sugar for sprinkling

Directions

To make the rhubarb jelly, cut the rhubarb into small pieces and place in a nonreactive pot. Add the sugar and the water. Cover and slowly bring to the boil. Reduce heat and gently simmer until the rhubarb is very soft, 15 to 20 minutes.

recipe continues . . .

Drain rhubarb in a fine-mesh strainer set over a bowl for at least 3 hours to obtain the maximum amount of juice.

Meanwhile, make the chocolate ganache. Place the broken chocolate in a heatproof bowl. Bring the cream to the boil and pour it over the chocolate. Stir with a whisk until the chocolate is melted and smooth. Evenly divide the ganache among 6 large martini glasses. Place them in the refrigerator to set, about 1 hour.

To finish the rhubarb jelly, place 2½ cups (600 mL) of the rhubarb juice in a nonreactive saucepan. Slowly warm the juice until very hot but not boiling. Squeeze the gelatin sheets in your hands to remove excess water, then add to the warm rhubarb juice. Stir until gelatin is dissolved. Pour the jelly evenly over the ganache. Return the glasses to the refrigerator to set, about 1 hour.

Meanwhile, make the maple cream. Simmer the maple syrup until reduced to ¼ cup (60 mL). Cool to room temperature.

Whip the cream until stiff. Fold in the reduced maple syrup. Top each glass with a thick layer of maple cream. Scrape a palette knife across the top of the glasses to smooth the cream. Refrigerate until ready to serve.

Garnish each glass with a little pile of rhubarb julienne, a mint sprig and a sprinkling of maple sugar. Serve.

Chilled Rhubarb Soup with Mint Meringues

Makes 6 servings

We are blessed with perennial rhubarb in Southern Ontario. It is so beautiful in its essence as a chilled dessert soup. Patrons of Empty Bowls, which always takes place in the spring, would be very upset if I decided to serve any soup other than this spring classic.

Ingredients

Meringue

4 egg whites

½ cup (100 g) granulated sugar

2 tablespoons (30 mL) chopped fresh mint

Rhubarb Soup

10 pounds (4.5 kg) fresh field-grown rhubarb

1 cup (200 g) granulated sugar

½ cup (125 mL) water

Garnish

3 tablespoons (50 mL) finely diced fresh
   field-grown rhubarb

3 tablespoons (50 mL) fresh field-grown rhubarb
   cut into julienne, held in cold water so it curls

2 tablespoons (30 mL) edible flower petals

Directions

The evening before serving, make the meringue. Preheat the oven to 160°F (70°C). Line a baking sheet with parchment paper.

Beat the egg whites until soft peaks form. Continue to beat while slowly adding the sugar until the meringue is stiff and shiny. Fold in the chopped mint. Spread the meringue to roughly ½ inch (1 cm) thick on the baking sheet and place in the oven overnight. By morning the meringue should be perfectly dry and without colour.

To make the rhubarb soup, cut the rhubarb into small pieces and place them in a large nonreactive pot. Add the sugar and water. Cover and slowly bring to the boil, then reduce heat and simmer, without stirring, until the rhubarb is very soft, approximately 15 minutes.

Suspend a cheesecloth-lined colander over a large bowl. Transfer the rhubarb mixture to the colander and let drain for 3 hours. Discard rhubarb. Refrigerate the soup for at least 6 hours.

For the garnish, in a small saucepan, cover the diced rhubarb with water. Simmer just until rhubarb is tender but not falling apart. Drain and refrigerate until needed.

Chill 6 bowls. Divide the cooked rhubarb pieces among the bowls. Ladle the chilled rhubarb soup into each bowl. Garnish each serving with some crumbled meringue, julienned rhubarb and a scattering of flower petals. Serve.

EMPTY BOWLS

I had been looking for a charity I could get behind that would benefit from the making and sharing of food. Empty Bowls started in the States. Sue Jeffries, a curator at Toronto's Gardiner Museum, approached me in '92 with the idea of recreating Empty Bowls in Canada, at the museum. It didn't take much to persuade me (and many other chefs). We've been donating soup to that event each year ever since. The beneficiary has always been Anishnawbe Health Toronto. Empty Bowls is the kind of event that a lot of people can get involved in. It's a collaboration between chefs, the Gardiner Museum and potters. The ticket is about $40. You get beautifully crafted soups from fifteen to twenty brilliant chefs from Toronto and you take home a unique hand-thrown pottery bowl. The potters donate all the bowls, the chefs bring the soup, the Gardiner provides the venue and all the money goes to the Anishnawbe. It's always sold out from day one. The event begins at five, but people start lining up at noon—they want to get first crack at those bowls!

Above: Chefs Alexandra Feswick, Scott Vivian and Marc Dufour

Above: Chef Mark Cutrara and Alexis Da Silva-Powell

Above: John Petcoff, Trish Donnelly and Renée Bellefeuille

Asparagus and Other Harbingers of Spring

The Asparagus Farm

Jo and I went to the asparagus farm down towards the Sandbanks, near Milford, in Prince Edward County. We hung out with Brian Beatty, the owner, who bent my ear for about an hour and a half. He is a weathered, chain-smoking, salt-of-the-earth farmer. He had first come to the County to play hockey, and after an injury benched him he stayed and started farming, working with another farmer until he was able to start his own place. After chatting a bit about the state of farming in this country, I finally persuaded him to let me ride his harvester and pick some asparagus.

I could barely spread my legs wide enough to sit in the harvester—it's almost like doing the splits, your legs are splayed right out. Your hands are free and you bend over at the waist between your legs. You have a knife, and when the asparagus comes along you just grab it; you move laterally clipping them off, gathering a bunch. Then when you get a moment or two, because the asparagus aren't coming constantly, you trim them and toss them into a box. They grade the spears later into No. 1s and No. 2s. Pencil asparagus is sometimes seen as more "gourmet," but I like the thicker asparagus. They just taste better.

We harvested some of Brian's asparagus and took it back to my farm. We set up my cast-iron cauldron over a fire. I assigned one of the guests to tend the fire. They never tell you this in fairy tales, but it takes a lot of intense heat to boil water in a cauldron. He got it, though, just kept building the fire and brought the water to the boil. We blanched the asparagus and I served it with a beurre blanc using Ontario hazelnuts. I had some porchetta on hand, like you do when you're a chef. Simple. Delish. It was a nice dinner. My dad came over, and Jo and my girlfriend, Victoria, were there along with Victoria's artist friends. Asparagus picked that day by me spread-eagled on a harvester, then cooked in a cauldron on a warm spring night. The embers glowed as the sun set.

Asparagus with Hazelnut Sauce

Makes 6 servings

For a present one Christmas, my cousin Anne gave me some hazelnuts grown in Ontario. She knows what a nut I am about local food. These hazelnuts were grown outside Port Hope. They were large, sweet and extremely flavourful. I managed to hold some back from the festivities and kept them in my refrigerator, just waiting for this lovely dish.

Ingredients

⅓ cup (75 g) hazelnuts

1 cup (250 mL) dry white wine

¼ cup (60 mL) cider vinegar

2 shallots, finely diced

2 teaspoons (10 g) cold butter, cut into small cubes

42 asparagus spears, peeled and trimmed to
　　7 inches (18 cm)

Directions

Preheat the oven to 350°F (180°C). Toast the hazelnuts on a small baking sheet until golden brown, about 10 minutes. Rub them in a tea towel to remove as much of the skins as possible. Let the nuts cool. Place the nuts in another clean tea towel, fold towel over, and crush with a rolling pin. Reserve.

In a small saucepan, combine the wine, vinegar and shallots. Bring to the boil over medium-high heat and reduce until the liquid is syrupy. Remove from the heat and whisk in the cold butter all at once until completely melted and the sauce is emulsified, returning the pot to the element briefly to help melt the butter. Whisk in the hazelnuts. Reserve at room temperature.

Bring a large pot of water to the boil. Add a generous pinch of salt. Add asparagus and cook until tender, about 4 minutes once the water returns to the boil.

Lay out 6 plates. Remove the asparagus from the water and arrange 7 spears on each plate in a pleasing manner. Spoon the toasted hazelnut sauce over the asparagus and serve.

45

Asparagus with Mustard Sabayon and Crunchy Shallots

Makes 6 servings

It is still early spring. I inspect the asparagus patch, pulling up young weeds and clearing last year's growth and oh, a purple-green shaft breaking the surface and oh! a couple more, and if it does not get too cold tonight, tomorrow when I come back here I might be able to harvest the first asparagus of the season. When asparagus is on, I can eat it every day. Nothing compares to its sweet freshness.

Ingredients

6 tablespoons (100 mL) clarified butter
4 shallots (3 thinly sliced and 1 roughly chopped)
Salt
¼ cup (60 mL) dry white wine
4 teaspoons (20 mL) white wine vinegar
2 bay leaves
3 egg yolks
Juice of ½ lemon
2 tablespoons (30 mL) Dijon mustard
42 thick asparagus spears, peeled and trimmed to
    7 inches (18 cm)

Directions

Melt the clarified butter in a saucepan over medium-low heat. Add the sliced shallots and gently fry them until they are golden but not too brown. Remove with a slotted spoon and transfer to paper towels to drain. Lightly salt them. Reserve the clarified butter at room temperature.

In a separate saucepan, place the white wine, white wine vinegar, bay leaves and chopped shallot. Bring to the boil, then reduce heat and gently reduce until syrupy. Strain this reduction into a stainless steel bowl. Whisk in the egg yolks.

In another saucepan, bring an inch or two of water to the boil over medium heat. Set the bowl with the egg yolks and reduction over the boiling water, whisking continuously. Occasionally take the bowl away from the heat while continuing to whisk to prevent the eggs from scrambling. Keep whisking, alternating briefly on and off the heat, until the "sabayon" is thick and frothy.

Turn off the heat. While whisking the sabayon over the water, add the reserved clarified butter in a slow, steady stream. Add the lemon juice and mustard. Whisk thoroughly. Season with salt. Remove the bowl from the pan and reserve at room temperature.

Meanwhile, bring a pot of water to the boil. Add a pinch of salt. Cook the asparagus until tender, about 4 minutes once the water returns to the boil.

While the asparagus is cooking, set out 6 plates. Pour a pool of mustard sabayon onto each plate. Remove the asparagus from the water and arrange 7 spears on each pool of sabayon. Sprinkle with the crunchy shallots and serve.

Asparagus Shooter with Chive Vinaigrette

Makes 6 servings

I read somewhere that the Queen said it was not only okay but proper to eat asparagus with one's fingers. I think that is the inspiration for this fun hors d'oeuvre. This recipe takes two of the first ingredients harvested each year and combines them for a taste explosion of spring.

Ingredients

1 egg yolk
1 teaspoon (5 mL) Dijon mustard
1 teaspoon (5 mL) cider vinegar
1 teaspoon (5 mL) lemon juice
Pinch of salt
¼ cup (60 mL) cold-pressed sunflower oil
1 tablespoon (15 mL) finely chopped fresh chives
18 asparagus spears, peeled and trimmed to
    3 inches (8 cm)

Directions

Bring a pot of water to the boil.

Meanwhile, in a blender, combine the egg yolk, mustard, cider vinegar, lemon juice and salt. Begin blending. When the ingredients are well blended, and while the blender is running, add the sunflower oil in a slow, steady stream. Add the chives and blend until the chlorophyll from the chives dyes the vinaigrette a pale shade of green. Divide the vinaigrette evenly among 6 shooter glasses.

Add a pinch of salt to the boiling water. Add the asparagus and boil for 3 minutes. Remove asparagus from the water and place 3 spears upside down into each shooter glass. Serve.

Asparagus in Wild Rice Crêpe

Makes 6 servings

Many years ago I was catering an event for a group of visiting Italians. It was spring and I wanted to give them something uniquely Canadian. It was a stand-up cocktail affair held outdoors in a walled garden. "Perfect!" I thought. I would bring my cauldron and suspend it over my portable wood-burning BBQ. That cauldron always seems to come out when asparagus is in season. I boiled water in the cauldron and cooked asparagus in front of the guests, then served the asparagus rolled in a wild rice flour crêpe. Tarragon provided a perfect herbal note to this warm asparagus canapé.

Ingredients

3 eggs, at room temperature
1¼ cups (300 mL) milk, at room temperature
Pinch of freshly grated nutmeg
Pinch of salt
¾ cup + 2 tablespoons (75 g) sifted pastry flour
2½ tablespoons (25 g) wild rice flour
½ cup (125 g) butter, melted and cooled to
    room temperature
18 asparagus spears, peeled and trimmed to
    about 4 inches (10 cm)
1 shallot, finely diced
2 tablespoons (30 mL) white wine vinegar
1 teaspoon (5 mL) chopped fresh tarragon
Salt and freshly ground black pepper

Directions

In a medium bowl, mix the eggs, milk, nutmeg and salt together with a whisk. While continuing to whisk, blend in the pastry flour, then the wild rice flour and finally ¼ cup (60 g) of the melted butter just until combined. The batter will probably look kind of lumpy. That's okay—it's better to have a few little lumps than to over-mix, which results in tough crêpes. Allow the crêpe batter to rest at room temperature for 1 hour.

Heat a small nonstick frying pan or crêpe pan (or 2 if you are feeling adventurous) over medium heat. Do not add any butter or oil to the pan. Add just enough batter to coat the bottom of the pan, swirling the pan to spread the batter as thinly as possible. Cook, turning once, until golden, about 1 minute. The first ones are always difficult and want to stick. Persevere and you will find your rhythm. You will need to make at least 6 crêpes. Set out your crêpes on the counter as they're cooked.

Bring a large pot of water to the boil and add a pinch of salt. Add the asparagus and cook for approximately 4 minutes after the water returns to the boil. Drain and transfer the asparagus to a bowl. Add the shallot, white wine vinegar, tarragon, the remaining ¼ cup (60 g) melted butter, and salt and pepper to taste; toss together well.

Place 3 spears on each crêpe, making sure to distribute the shallots evenly. Roll up the crêpes with the asparagus inside like a cigar. Serve while still warm as an hors d'oeuvre.

Spring Minestrone with Black Walnut and Arugula Pesto

Makes 6 servings

The black walnut is a native Ontario ingredient. The tree is well suited to our climate and can be found across the province and into Quebec. The black walnut has much more pronounced savoury characteristics than its English cousin.

Ingredients

½ cup (125 mL) cooked white beans

1 carrot, quartered lengthwise and thinly sliced

1 celery stalk, diced

1 leek, halved lengthwise and thinly sliced

6 asparagus spears, peeled and thinly sliced
   on the bias

2 bay leaves

12 cups (3 L) vegetable stock

1 teaspoon (5 mL) roughly chopped fresh thyme

12 black peppercorns, coarsely ground

Salt

6 arugula leaves

2 tablespoons (30 mL) black walnut pieces

2 tablespoons (30 mL) finely grated
   Parmigiano-Reggiano

¼ cup (60 mL) fine olive oil

Directions

In a large soup pot, combine the beans, carrot, celery, leek, asparagus, bay leaves and vegetable stock. Bring to the boil, then reduce heat and simmer for 15 minutes. Add the thyme, peppercorns and salt to taste, and simmer for 2 more minutes. Discard the bay leaves.

Meanwhile, in a food processor, combine the arugula, walnuts, cheese and olive oil. Blend into a pesto.

Lay out 6 bowls. Ladle the soup into the bowls. Top each serving with a nice dollop of the pesto. Serve.

55

Wild Leek and Potato Gratin

Makes 6 servings

Out walking in the forest in late April, you can still see your breath. The snow has mostly receded. The forest floor is carpeted in green. The smell of chopped garlic fills the air. You look down and realize you're walking on wild leeks! Right there beside the trilliums. In fact, their leaf structure is almost identical. Like every good hunter, you are also a conservationist. You don't clear-cut the wild leeks. Rather, you harvest selectively as you move through, leaving much behind to enjoy in the years to come.

The distinctive flavour of the wild leek lends itself well to potatoes. This dish is a delicious combination of a root vegetable that has been stored over the winter and the first greens of spring.

Ingredients

2 pounds (1 kg) potatoes (any kind), peeled
  and thinly sliced
¾ cup (175 mL) fresh wild leeks sliced on the
  bias as thinly as possible
½ cup (125 mL) grated 2-year-old cheddar
1 tablespoon (15 mL) butter
1 tablespoon (15 mL) roughly chopped
  fresh thyme
¼ teaspoon (1 mL) freshly grated nutmeg
Salt and freshly ground black pepper
2 cups (500 mL) whipping cream

Directions

Preheat the oven to 250°F (120°C). Butter a 9-inch (2.5 L) square baking dish.

In a medium bowl, stir together the potatoes, leeks, cheddar, butter, thyme, nutmeg, and salt and pepper to taste. Evenly layer the potato mixture in the baking dish, pouring some cream over each layer as you go.

Cover with foil and bake for about 2½ hours, until a wooden skewer passes easily through the potatoes.

Preheat the broiler. Remove the foil and brown the gratin, moving it around until the top is evenly golden brown. Serve.

57

Beet-Pickled Wild Leeks

Makes four 1-pint (500 mL) jars

Working with fresh wild leeks for about two precious weeks is a welcome inspiration each spring. Don't forget to preserve some for year-round use; wait till the end of the season, when the bulbs are at their largest. We include a piece of beet to add colour.

Ingredients

1 small red beet, peeled and quartered
8 cups (2 L) wild leeks, roots and leaves trimmed
4 cups (1 L) pickling brine (see recipe page 287)

Directions

For canning instructions, see pages 282–83.

Place a quarter of a beet in each of 4 sterilized 1-pint (500 mL) mason jars. Pack the wild leeks into the jars, up to the neck.

Bring the brine to a boil and pour into each jar, leaving ½-inch (1 cm) headspace but making sure the leeks are covered. Seal jars and process in boiling water for 15 minutes. Cool on the counter and store in a cool, dark place.

Local Food Movement Dinners

I have been doing something called Local Food Movement Dinners in one form or another since 2004 or so.

Immediately following the restructuring of my company, after J.K. Wine Bar was severed off and I went from employing 140 people to employing 40, those of us who survived ended up at Gilead with a mandate to turn the company into something that was "cash positive." We put a lot of creative thinking into making what we were passionate about into something remunerative for the company. What bobbed to the surface was an idea that eventually became the Local Food Movement Dinner series.

The idea was to invite people from our community—our suppliers—to come to the restaurant and tell their stories as artisanal food producers, cheese-makers, winemakers, specialty beef farmers, pork farmers, lamb farmers . . . The criteria for involvement was that they be located somewhere around Toronto, operating on a small scale and dealing directly with us, not through any middle person. We were really attempting to build a sense of food culture in Toronto, and give folks the opportunity to connect with one another in new ways.

We did one dinner with Matchbox Gardens, a local produce and seed company. I think the Local Food Movement Dinner series captures that new thinking of the very-small-footprint operation. You have a small staff and you're all very passionate about what you're doing. At that dinner we paired the food with Marynissen wines. The late John Marynissen was one of Ontario's wine pioneers. One of the visionaries in the '70s, he was the first to grow vinifera grapes in Niagara.

Local Food Movement
Dinner—Spring Feast

Essence Forestière

Makes 6 servings

I walk back into the woodlot. It is the part of my farm property that is low-lying. In the fall and spring it is pretty wet, and in the summer it is thick with mosquitoes. Typically a farm property like mine has a section given over to managed forest. This is the source of wood for building on the property and for firewood. Every twenty-five years or so, a farmer may have an arborist come in and assess how many logs could be taken out to maintain the healthy balance of trees for the area. It is in the woodlot, during the spring and fall, that I will most often spot mushrooms. I love the earthy smells and intense quiet of the woodlot. It is like an outdoor cathedral.

Wild mushrooms are quite common in our wooded areas. Of course, extreme caution must be exercised when harvesting. While there are detailed books on the subject of mycology, it is best to go foraging with an experienced person who can help to identify the good and the bad. Don't take chances on your own!

Ingredients

1 pound (500 g) pheasant back or other wild
    mushrooms, roughly chopped
1 onion, finely chopped
1 carrot, finely chopped
1 leek, halved lengthwise and chopped
2 celery stalks, finely chopped
2 tablespoons (30 mL) tomato paste
1 tablespoon (15 mL) roughly chopped
    fresh thyme
½ teaspoon (2 mL) freshly grated nutmeg
12 black peppercorns, coarsely ground
2 bay leaves
6 egg whites
12 cups (3 L) vegetable stock
Salt
2 green onions, thinly sliced on the bias

Directions

In a large soup pot, combine the wild mushrooms, onion, carrot, leek, celery, tomato paste, thyme, nutmeg, ground peppercorns, bay leaves and egg whites. Mix well. Add the vegetable stock and mix again.

Slowly bring to the boil, stirring regularly. As the egg whites begin to coagulate, all the ingredients will fuse together to form a "raft." The raft is essential to obtaining a clear essence or consommé. Once the raft has formed, reduce the heat to a simmer. Simmer the essence for approximately 1 hour.

Strain the essence through a fine-mesh strainer. Do not press on the solids. Discard the solids. Season with salt to taste.

Wipe out the pot and return the essence to it. Bring just to the boil. Place sliced green onion in each of 6 bowls and ladle the essence into the bowls. Serve.

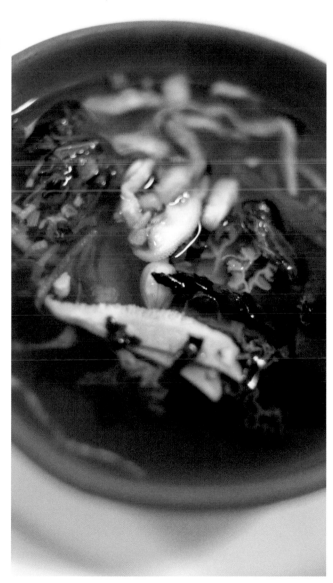

Eggs

Murray the Egg Man

In 2010 this fellow approached me at an event where I was participating. He said that he was living in the city and he wasn't enjoying his life; he said he just loved farming and he wanted to get back to that. He wanted to raise chickens, a whole bunch of different breeds, and harvest multicoloured eggs. I asked him to call me once he got started.

About two years later he approached me again and told me he was producing eggs now and wanted to know if I'd buy some. I told him to send them over. The first box that came, the flat on top had eggs all with different coloured shells—some pale blue, some cream, some brown, some pale green—and he'd arranged them so they stood in contrast and spelled out my initials, JK. We've been buying from Murray ever since.

We use his eggs for everything. They are completely organic and they are from at least twelve different breeds.

We are at such a disadvantage in this country when it comes to knowing eggs. If a young chef leaves Canada and heads to Europe, lands in a grand kitchen, and the head chef orders the classic test—"cook the perfect omelette"—that young cook from here is up against it. Real farm-fresh eggs behave so much differently from the average, months-old supermarket egg; they're stronger and thicker, not watery. Making an omelette with a farm-fresh egg is such a pleasure; you don't have to fight it.

That's why I deal with someone like Murray and use only his eggs. I know that those eggs are no older than three days. We pay twice as much, but it's worth it.

Long before it was trendy, Chef Kennedy was quietly helping to change the way people ate and thought about food, simply by making changes in the way he operated his kitchen. He made a choice years ago to create relationships with his suppliers and to think about how to obtain the best local products, by helping to support small-scale operations.

One of Chef Kennedy's greatest accomplishments has been in creating relationships that support the growth of an alternative food system—becoming a champion of the individuals who work the farms and the fields and allowing them to grow their own businesses.

ARLENE STEIN, CHAIR, TERROIR HOSPITALITY INDUSTRY SYMPOSIUM

Devilled Organic Eggs

Makes 10 devilled eggs

When I think of devilled eggs I picture a red-checked tablecloth over a picnic table in some bucolic setting by a stream. They are perfect picnic food, because the preparation is all done before you leave the house.

At Gilead I serve these for lunch with crisp toast and vegetarian dips.

Ingredients

5 hard-boiled organic eggs
½ teaspoon (2 mL) English dry mustard
½ teaspoon (2 mL) white wine vinegar
1 teaspoon (5 mL) honey
¼ teaspoon (1 mL) chili vinegar
Juice of ¼ lemon
2 tablespoons (30 g) butter, softened
1 tablespoon (15 mL) cider mayonnaise
   (see recipe page 348)
Salt
Sweet Spanish paprika for garnishing

Directions

Peel the eggs and cut in half lengthwise. Remove the yolks and place in a bowl, setting the whites aside. In another bowl, mix the dry mustard and white wine vinegar into a paste, then add to the egg yolks. Add the honey, chili vinegar and lemon juice. Mix with an electric mixer. Beat in the softened butter and mayonnaise. Add salt to taste. Whip until light and fluffy. Chill for 1 hour.

Put the yolk mixture into a piping bag fitted with a star tip and pipe into the egg whites. Garnish with sweet Spanish paprika.

Poached Egg on Quinoa and Bean Salad

Makes 4 servings

I like to eat well at lunch, and this dish is hearty and rich, with a really nice combination of fresh and dried beans.

Ingredients

3½ ounces (100 g) fresh green or yellow beans
1 cup (250 mL) cooked quinoa (any colour)
1 cup (250 mL) cooked white, black or
    kidney beans
2 shallots, finely chopped
3 tablespoons (50 mL) white wine vinegar
1 tablespoon (15 mL) roughly chopped
    fresh summer savory
Salt and freshly ground black pepper
4 eggs
4 crisp toasts, if desired
¼ cup (60 mL) fine olive oil

Directions

Cook the green beans in boiling salted water for about 5 minutes. Drain, refresh under cold water and drain again. Cut the beans on the bias and place in a medium bowl. Add the quinoa, white beans, shallots, 2 tablespoons (30 mL) of the white wine vinegar, savory, and salt and pepper to taste. Mix well. Divide the quinoa and bean salad among 4 salad plates.

Bring a saucepan of water to the boil; add the remaining 1 tablespoon (15 mL) white wine vinegar. Reduce the heat to a simmer. Break the eggs into the simmering water one at a time and poach until they are set but not hard-cooked, approximately 3 minutes. Transfer the eggs one at a time with a slotted spoon onto paper towels to drain.

Garnish each salad with a poached egg set atop a piece of crisp toast. Drizzle with the olive oil and season with salt and pepper. Serve.

Blue Cheese and Leek Tart

Makes 6 servings

The secret to this recipe is in the freshly grated nutmeg. That little bit of warm spice elevates all the flavours and turns a simple recipe into a killer dish.

Ingredients

8 ounces (250 g) pie pastry
  (use your favourite recipe)
4 eggs
4 cups (1 L) 10% cream
⅛ teaspoon (0.5 mL) freshly grated nutmeg
Salt and freshly ground black pepper
2 cups (500 mL) leeks sliced into thin strips
1 cup (125 g) crumbled artisanal blue cheese
  from Ontario or Quebec

Directions

Preheat the oven to 350°F (180°C).

Grease a 14- × 4-inch (35 × 10 cm) rectangular or 9-inch (23 cm) round tart pan with removable bottom.

Roll out the pastry into a rectangle slightly larger than your tart pan. Fit the pastry into the pan and trim the edges. Line with parchment paper or foil and fill with baking weights. Bake until edge is pale golden, 20 to 30 minutes. Remove parchment and weights, then bake until edge is golden brown and crust looks dry, another 15 minutes. Remove from the oven. Reduce oven temperature to 325°F (160°C).

In a bowl, combine the eggs, cream, nutmeg, and salt and pepper to taste. Whisk thoroughly. Arrange the sliced leeks and crumbled blue cheese in the tart shell. Pour the egg mixture over the leeks and cheese. Bake until the filling has set, approximately 25 minutes. Test for doneness by gently shaking the tart. The filling should be set and slightly puffed up. Cool on a rack for 10 minutes before serving.

summer

DURING THE SUMMER ON THE FARM WE ARE

TENDING THE VINEYARD, WEEDING THE GARDEN,

HARVESTING LETTUCES AND HERBS FOR THE

DINNER TABLE, SHELLING PEAS ON THE PORCH

AND SIPPING G&T'S IN THE BALMY TWILIGHT

WHILE WE WATCH THE SUN SET

OVER THE WOODLOT.

Steamed Greens with Chili Oil and Toasted Garlic

Makes 6 servings

This recipe offers a great opportunity to use leafy green vegetables. Use any greens you have at hand. Currently I like to use spinach, kale, Swiss chard, nettles, lamb's quarters and rapini.

Ingredients

¾ cup (175 mL) fine olive oil

1 teaspoon (5 mL) chili flakes

1 teaspoon (5 mL) sweet paprika

3 cloves garlic, thinly sliced

2 bunches of spinach or other leafy green, washed and dried

Flaky sea salt

Directions

In a small bowl, stir 6 tablespoons (90 mL) of the olive oil with the chili flakes and paprika. Allow to sit at room temperature overnight.

The next day, strain the mixture through a coffee filter. Reserve oil.

Place a medium frying pan over medium heat. Add the remaining 6 tablespoons (90 mL) olive oil. Add the garlic and gently fry, stirring from time to time, until golden and crisp. Remove from the oil and reserve. Reserve the oil for another use.

Set up a steamer over high heat. When the water is boiling, add the spinach, cover and steam for about 5 minutes.

Meanwhile, set out 6 plates. Divide the spinach evenly among the plates. Sprinkle each serving with the toasted garlic, the chili oil and a sprinkling of sea salt. Serve.

Pickled Okra

Makes six 1-pint (500 mL) jars

One of the major reasons for the gastronomic uniqueness of Southern Ontario is the cultural diversity of our population. We are discovering ingredients that are from other cultures that have not traditionally been grown here. Okra is a good example. Traditionally used in the Caribbean, Africa and the southern United States, it flourishes in our hot, humid Ontario summers. I plant it each year with great results. An added bonus is the incredibly beautiful flower it produces.

Ingredients

5 pounds (2.2 kg) fresh okra

6 small red serrano chilies

6 tablespoons (90 mL) fine olive oil

8 cups (2 L) pickling brine (see recipe page 287)

Directions

For canning instructions, see pages 282–83.

Preheat the broiler. Line a baking sheet with foil. Spread the okra evenly on the baking sheet. Broil, turning occasionally, until soft and slightly charred all over.

Pack the okra into 6 sterilized 1-pint (500 mL) mason jars. To each jar, add 1 chili and 1 tablespoon (15 mL) olive oil. Pour brine into each jar, stopping ½ inch (1 cm) from the rim. Seal jars and process in boiling water for 15 minutes. Cool on the counter and store in a cool, dark place.

Ratatouille

Makes 6 servings

This dish epitomizes summer. I feel the heat beating down and the air shimmers off the garden. Most of the mosquitoes have decamped—certainly their numbers have mercifully decreased. Harvesting is becoming a pleasure. I have planted garlic, onions, peppers, tomatoes, eggplant, zucchini and basil. Garlic is already curing in the barn. The remainder of the vegetables lie waiting in the field. I will harvest the vegetables, then prepare the ratatouille this afternoon and serve it for dinner. Like any stew, it benefits from, to paraphrase Mark Twain, letting the flavours swap around awhile before tucking in.

Ingredients

6 tablespoons (90 mL) fine olive oil
2 medium onions, cut into large dice
4 cloves garlic, finely minced
1 eggplant, cut into large dice
2 zucchini, cut into large dice
4 ripe red tomatoes, seeded and cut into large dice
9 fresh basil leaves, cut into thin strips

Directions

Place a large saucepan over medium heat. Add the olive oil. Add the onions and garlic and gently sweat in the oil for 3 minutes. Stir in the eggplant and zucchini and gently sweat everything for 30 minutes, stirring from time to time.

Add the tomatoes and continue to cook for an additional 5 minutes. Stir in the basil, then remove from the heat. Allow to rest for 2 hours at room temperature. Reheat before serving.

Swiss Chard Pie

Makes 8 servings

I feel lucky to have some land in Prince Edward County. The area used to be known as the garden of Canada. The limestone soil gives so much flavour and dimension to all the fruits and vegetables that I have tasted from here. My plan is to grow enough of certain things for the restaurant to use while they're in season. I've been focusing on garlic, asparagus, onions, shallots, peppers, tomatoes and potatoes. Once in a while I will plant half a row of something to try it out. I've discovered that Swiss chard grows extremely well in my garden. My kitchen at Gilead is in chard from July through to the end of October. I'm gobsmacked by how much of it there is and am inspired to find other applications for it other than sautéing or braising. This recipe is adapted from a classic sweet tart popular in the south of France called *tarte aux blettes*.

Although I call for a 9-inch (23 cm) pie plate here, I often make this in a rectangular tart form for large events as it's much easier to portion.

Ingredients

1 disc (8 ounces/250 g) sweet pastry
   (see recipe page 153)
16 Swiss chard leaves, 3 inches (8 cm)
   of stem left on
6 eggs
½ cup + 2 tablespoons (125 g) granulated sugar
3½ ounces (100 g) peeled roasted chestnuts
⅔ cup (100 g) raisins
Zest of 1 lemon
½ teaspoon (2 mL) freshly grated nutmeg
2 whole cloves, ground in a mortar and pestle
¼ stick cinnamon, grated
Pinch of salt
1 egg, lightly beaten, for egg wash

Directions

Preheat the oven to 350°F (180°C).

Roll out the pastry into a disc about ⅛ inch (3 mm) thick and fit it into a 9-inch (23 cm) pie plate. Trim the overhang, leaving ½ inch (1 cm), then fold overhang under. Gather trim and remaining pastry into a ball; wrap in plastic. Refrigerate pastry shell and extra pastry until firm, approximately 30 minutes.

recipe continues . . .

91

Line the pastry shell with parchment or foil and fill with baking weights. Bake until edge is light golden, about 15 minutes. Remove parchment and weights, then bake until crust looks dry, another 10 to 15 minutes. Transfer to a cooling rack, but leave the oven on.

Meanwhile, blanch the Swiss chard in a large pot of boiling water for 2 minutes, then transfer it to a colander to drain. Lay it out on tea towels to air-cool. When it's cool enough to handle, squeeze out excess water and finely chop.

In a medium bowl, whisk together the eggs and sugar until light and fluffy. Add the Swiss chard, chestnuts, raisins, lemon zest, nutmeg, cloves, cinnamon and salt. Spread the filling evenly in the pie shell. Roll out the reserved dough to ⅛-inch (3 mm) thickness, then cut into strips 1 inch (2.5 cm) wide. Weave strips in a lattice pattern on top of the pie. Press the ends of the lattice against the baked pie shell and trim the edges; brush lattice with the egg wash. Bake until lattice is golden brown and the filling is set, approximately 1 hour. Cool on a rack. Serve with vanilla ice cream.

92

The Hillier Fish Fry

The Hillier Fish Fry is a community event for the people of Prince Edward County. My involvement started in 2001, when my neighbour, who was on the local recreation committee, was put in charge of organizing the event. I told him I'd like to be the caterer for it. Tickets sold for ten dollars each, and he asked if I could work within that budget. I said sure, because I was more interested in making a contribution to the community than making a profit. So I asked him, "What does a guest get for ten dollars?"

He replied, "Oh, they get fish, they get fries, they get tartar sauce, they get coleslaw, they get a bun and they get butter. Oh, and they get pie. And they get coffee."

My menu probably didn't read much differently from the previous years'. It was a simple menu, but the provenance of the meal's ingredients and the way it was executed set it apart from the experience of previous years. People noticed, and I felt very gratified by that.

It was held in June, so we foraged for wild leeks for the tartar sauce. I asked the recreation committee ladies if they could go out and harvest rhubarb for the dessert. I made apple strudel with fresh-churned vanilla ice cream and used the rhubarb in a strawberry rhubarb compote. The first year I cooked halibut, but once I had met the local fishers I switched to pickerel or perch for the following years.

I've been doing the fish fry for nine years, and every year the crowds kept growing until we capped it at five hundred tickets. The event has become a signature community event for my little village of Hillier. Its success proves that people respond positively to the genuine experience of locally sourced food prepared with care.

Jamie, right away when he came here, he threw himself into the community. When they first asked him to do the Hillier Fish Fry it was pretty funny because they didn't really know who he was. He threw a dinner for the community when he first moved out here, a beautiful dinner, completely out of his own pocket. It reminded me of Babette's Feast *because everyone was there but they really didn't know who this guy was. They knew he was from the city, but like all the old Danes in the movie sitting there thinking "I will not like this, I will not like this!" they didn't know if they'd like his highfalutin food or what to expect. Then you started hearing laughter and people just enjoying themselves. They didn't know whether they'd like this fancy food or what, they just knew it was good and the whole town hall was completely abuzz.*

GEOFF HEINRICKS, WINEMAKER AND AUTHOR

Tempura Pickerel with Wild Leek Tartar Sauce

Makes 6 servings

After the first fish fry, I received a few letters from people who had attended, thanking me. One letter I remember said, "You brought tears to my eyes. These are taste memories that I have from my childhood of my father out on the back porch churning ice cream with milk from our dairy cows." My simple menu reminded so many guests of how their mothers and grandmothers had cooked. I realized that food doesn't have to be fancy to be memorable. In fact, sometimes it is the simplest things that resonate most. This recipe uses fresh local fish and a twist on the traditional tartar sauce.

Ingredients

2 cups (500 mL) cider mayonnaise
  (see recipe page 348)
5 beet-pickled wild leeks (see recipe page 59),
  finely chopped
1 tablespoon (15 mL) chopped fresh parsley
1 tablespoon (15 mL) finely chopped fresh chives
1 tablespoon (15 mL) chopped capers
1 teaspoon (5 mL) lemon juice
Salt and freshly ground black pepper
12 slices (2 ounces/60 g each) fresh skinless
  pickerel fillet (any white fish will do in a pinch)
4 cups (1 L) sunflower oil
½ cup (125 mL) all-purpose flour
½ cup (125 mL) cornstarch
1½ cups (375 mL) cold club soda
Lemon wedges for garnishing

Directions

In a bowl, mix the cider mayonnaise, wild leeks, parsley, chives, capers, lemon juice, and salt and pepper to taste. Reserve.

Season the pickerel fillets with salt and leave to "cure" for 15 minutes.

Meanwhile, in a large soup pot over medium heat, heat the sunflower oil to 350°F (180°C).

To make the tempura batter, whisk together the flour and cornstarch in a medium bowl. Add the cold club soda and a pinch of salt. Mix well using a whisk.

Working with three or four fillets at a time, run the fillets through the tempura batter and fry in the oil until golden brown, 3 to 4 minutes. Drain on paper towels.

Lay out 6 plates. Place 2 fillets on each plate with a generous spoonful of the wild leek tartar sauce. Garnish with a lemon wedge. Serve.

Cole Slaw

Makes 8 servings

I'm taken back to the kitchens of the Windsor Arms Hotel. A Dickensian basement with labyrinthine corridors filled with dripping pipes and dread. An Austrian sous-chef admonishing me because I haven't salted and squeezed the cabbage before making cole slaw. "Here, *stift*, I'm going to show you," he said, using the German word for apprentice. He sliced the cabbage thinly, then tossed it with salt and caraway seeds. He told me to let it rest for about a half-hour, then rinse it in cold water, then squeeze it out. I was struck with how the cabbage became so much more pliable and dense, far less watery. The caraway must be an eastern European addition. Needless to say, I have been making cole slaw the same way ever since.

Ingredients

1 small green cabbage

1 medium carrot

Salt

½ teaspoon (2 mL) caraway seeds

⅓ cup (75 mL) white wine vinegar

¼ cup (60 mL) honey

¼ cup (60 mL) cold-pressed sunflower oil

Directions

Shred the cabbage and carrot as thinly as possible. Spread out on a baking sheet and sprinkle generously with salt and the caraway seeds. Allow to rest for 30 minutes. Rinse thoroughly in cold water. Using your hands, squeeze out as much water from handfuls of carrot and cabbage as you can. Place the handfuls as you go into a large bowl.

Add the white wine vinegar, honey and sunflower oil; toss well. Taste and add more salt if necessary.

Reception in the Vineyard, Dinner in the Barn

It was June 2013 and I was already up in the vineyard. I had a trailer that I pulled up there with the tractor. All of the sparkling wine and flutes and all the hors d'oeuvres were laid out on the trailer. I had a fire set up and I was grilling lamb as the guests began to arrive. It was beautiful.

Then the heavens opened up and it just poured. One of those crazy summer showers that comes out of nowhere, soaks everything and disappears in five minutes. It rained so hard in this short period of time that the flutes were half full with rain water. Jo and I just shook out the water and poured the wine. People were amazingly okay with that. It's all part of being on the farm; people feel like that's part of the deal. It behooves us all to just go with it.

When I'm not catering an event, I usually put people to work when they come for dinner at the farm. It's part of how we do things there, it's more inclusive, to bring people in and have a conversation rather than be segregated off doing the cooking on my own while everyone is outside having a party. So at the farm we get everyone helping. I like to outsource veg prep, shucking corn, peeling carrots, harvesting tomatoes or chard.

There are always cocktails. Lately we have been excited about exploring the artisanal production of gin in Prince Edward County. There might be gin and tonics for everyone, garnished with a fragrant sprig of lovage. If it's sunny we sit out on the deck—it's just beautiful. Nothing fancy, the farm is very rustic. Victoria and I are always working on it, making it more bright and airy, and welcoming. There are two houses. The main house has the plumbing and the kitchen, and that's where we gather. My house is in the back. There's no plumbing, but there is electricity. My goal is, in the very near future, to actually put an addition on that house so that it has a kitchen and bathroom in it. Those are nice things to have in a house, right?

GASTRONOMY ON THE FARM
WITH JAMIE KENNEDY
SATURDAY JUNE 1ST, 2013

HORS D'ŒUVRES

·MARINATED PICKEREL ROLL-UP
·TEA DEVILED EGGS
·DUCK LIVER MOUSSE ON OAT TOAST
·CLASSIC BEEF TARTARE ON BRIOCHE ROUND
·GRILLED LAMB CEVAPCICI
2009 Hinterland Les Étoiles
Prince Edward County VQA

MENU

* * * * *

SPRING SALAD WITH ROASTED SHALLOT & CHIVE VINAIGRETTE

* * * * *

GREAT LAKES CHOWDER WITH ASPARAGUS

* * * * *

CONFIT SUCKLING PORCHETTA WITH CIDER-POACHED APPLES

* * * * *

GRAND PRIX WINNING CHEESES
·TASTING NOTES COURTESY OF DAIRY FARMERS OF CANADA

* * * * *

RHUBARB SOUP WITH
FRESH BELLA CASARA RICOTTA CANNOLO

* * * * *

COFFEE OR TEA

I've been lucky to go to Jamie's farm for several visits over the years, and can see a veil of calm and contentment come down over him whenever he's there. The forecast was not looking good for the cocktail reception in the vineyard, but Jamie is pretty darn stubborn about following through on his vision, so he steamed ahead. I remember asking him, "What if it rains?" to which he replied, "It's not going to." Thank goodness it was just warm enough to still feel comfortable even while soaking wet!

JO DICKINS, ASSISTANT, PHOTOGRAPHER

Marinated Pickerel

Makes 2 fillets

This is another example of taking a classic recipe from another culture—in this case gravlax from Sweden—and adapting it to locally available ingredients. Try this with the fennel and onion salad on page 212, as in the photo, to make marinated pickerel roll-ups.

Ingredients
Cure
2¼ pounds (1 kg) coarse sea salt
2¼ pounds (1 kg) granulated sugar
1 bunch of fresh dill, chopped
1 bunch of fresh coriander, chopped
3 tablespoons (50 mL) black peppercorns, crushed
3 tablespoons (50 mL) coriander seeds, crushed
2 fresh skin-on pickerel fillets

Paste
½ bunch of fresh dill, finely chopped
½ bunch of fresh coriander, finely chopped
2 tablespoons (30 mL) crushed black peppercorns

Directions
To cure the pickerel, in a baking pan or plastic bin large enough to hold the fillets in one layer, mix together well the salt, sugar, dill, fresh coriander, peppercorns and coriander seeds. Completely submerge the fillets in the salt mixture. Cover and leave in the fridge overnight.

The next day, remove the fillets from the cure and rinse under cold water. Pat dry. Discard the cure mixture.

To make the paste, stir together the dill, fresh coriander and peppercorns. Press the paste on the top of each fillet. If possible, refrigerate overnight before serving. The fillets will keep for 2 weeks in the refrigerator.

To serve, thinly slice fillets on the diagonal (as you would for smoked salmon), leaving skin behind, and enjoy with a hearty bread such as rye or pumpernickel, some crème fraîche and fresh dill.

Lettuces with Roasted Shallot Vinaigrette

Makes 6 servings

Growing lettuces at the farm means I have fresh leaves to pick for dinner every night. Pick a few leaves here and there and the plant will keep producing all summer long. At the dinner in the barn, we served this salad with an early-season garnish of carrots and semi-cured tomatoes (see recipe page 137). It's a very versatile salad.

Ingredients

6 shallots, cut in quarters lengthwise
1 small head of Boston lettuce
1 small head of red oak leaf lettuce
1 bunch of arugula
2 egg yolks
7 fluid ounces (200 mL) white wine vinegar
Juice of 1 lemon
2 tablespoons (30 mL) Dijon mustard
2 tablespoons (30 mL) honey
2 cups (500 mL) cold-pressed sunflower oil
Salt
1 small fennel bulb, thinly sliced
2 radishes, thinly sliced

Directions

Preheat the oven to 325°F (160°C). Place the shallots on a baking sheet and roast until very soft but not caramelized, about 30 minutes.

Meanwhile, break the lettuces and arugula into bite-size pieces into a sink full of cold water.

In a blender, combine the egg yolks, vinegar, lemon juice, mustard and honey. Add the roasted shallots. Begin blending on high speed. Continue to blend while adding the sunflower oil in a slow, steady stream. Season with salt.

Dry the lettuces and divide among 6 plates. Sprinkle each salad with the sliced fennel and sliced radishes. Drizzle each salad with the roasted shallot vinaigrette. Serve.

Pressed Perch Terrine with Watercress Purée and Beet-Pickled Wild Leeks

Makes 20 servings

Perch is just one of the truly delicious fish coming out of the Great Lakes. I get mine from Steph Purdy and her family. They have run Purdy's Fisheries, a fishing fleet and fish-and-chip shop, on the shores of Lake Huron for more than a hundred years. This terrine is an excellent accompaniment to Great Lakes Chowder (see recipe page 162). In the photo (page 117) it is shown served on the chowder with a fleuron (puff pastry) garnish.

This recipe makes a large number of servings, but leftovers are easily frozen for future use. To make the terrine you will need a 6-cup (1.5 L) oval or rectangular enamelled cast-iron or porcelain terrine mould with a lid, or a metal loaf pan.

Ingredients

2 pounds (1 kg) fresh skin-on yellow perch fillets
1 clove garlic, finely minced
1 teaspoon (5 mL) roughly chopped fresh tarragon
1 teaspoon (5 mL) pastis or other anise liqueur
Salt
2 bunches of fresh watercress, large stems removed
1 bunch of fresh watercress for garnishing
½ jar (1 pint/500 mL) beet-pickled wild leeks
   (see recipe page 59)

Directions

Preheat the oven to 300°F (150°C).

Carefully remove the skin from each perch fillet, working from the tail end. Reserve the fillets and skin. In a medium bowl, mix together the garlic, tarragon, pastis and salt to taste. Add the perch fillets and gently toss to coat.

Butter a small lidded terrine mould or a metal loaf pan. Line the bottom and sides with the perch skins, slightly overlapping and leaving an overhang of about 2 inches (5 cm) on each side. Layer the fillets of perch in the terrine, packing tightly.

recipe continues . . .

Cover the terrine and set it in a baking dish; add hot water to come halfway up the sides. Poach the terrine until the interior temperature reaches 130°F (55°C), about 45 minutes. Remove terrine from the water. Remove the lid and cover the surface with plastic wrap. Place a heavy jar (of pickles, for example) on top to weigh down ("press") the terrine. Cool overnight in the refrigerator.

Before serving, bring a large pot of water to the boil. Add the 2 bunches of watercress leaves and cook for about 2 minutes. Drain. Transfer the warm watercress to a blender and purée. Season with salt.

Pour a small pool of watercress purée onto salad plates. Unmould the perch terrine onto a cutting board and cut into thin, even slices using a sharp bread knife. Place 1 slice on each pool of watercress purée. Garnish with fresh watercress leaves and beet-pickled wild leeks. Serve.

Terrine will keep for about 1 week in the refrigerator, or freeze for up to 3 months.

When I was a kid peeling potatoes in a restaurant you've never heard of, I was a giant fan of Jamie Kennedy's. I'd never met him—it would be twenty years before I'd get the chance. When I came to Toronto in 2012, I went for lunch with Bonnie Stern at Gilead Café. It was possibly the best meal I had in 2012. I had a simple lunch. I had the best cheeseburger I've ever had. I had the best beet salad I've ever had. I had the best green salad I've ever had. I loved the room. I loved the utter simplicity of the space. I loved his little Prince Edward County white wine he makes.

Jamie Kennedy is one of the most important chefs in Canada of the last fifty years. Period. What was Canadian food until forty years ago? Jamie Kennedy is someone we've all respected since day one. He's so much more of a real chef than I am. Seeing the guy with the dirty-ass apron come up to shake my hand with his own beet juice–stained hands at one o'clock in the afternoon at lunch on a Tuesday at Gilead Café—that's a real chef for you.

He's been to Joe Beef once. Fred Morin had the honour of cooking for him, and it was a big deal for Fred. We messaged back and forth thirty times as he ate. We'd both been longing to have contact with him or wanted some kind of validation from him for our own careers. For real. There's Michael Stadtländer, Normand Laprise and Jamie Kennedy. The end. When we were kids that was it. We're well studied in their careers—as studied as we are on any other famous chef's—their body of work. Kennedy's always been analyzed very closely by us. He's an amazing chef. Amazing.

DAVE MCMILLAN, CHEF AND CO-OWNER OF JOE BEEF, LIVERPOOL HOUSE AND LE VIN PAPILLON

Local Food Movement
Dinner—Jazz Night

Curried Sweet Potato Soup with Raita

Makes 6 servings

I remember getting off the airplane in Colombo, Sri Lanka, with my mum. I was twenty years old and I had never seen a palm tree. The air was thick and sultry, the smells, exotic and new. Our taxi driver on the way in from the airport wore a sarong and white shirt, no shoes. We shared the road with pedestrians and bulla carts and horses and water buffaloes. Our driver pressed through, using the horn as an instrument of driving. I was fascinated and terrified all at once. I glanced over at my mum, who was coming back to the island for the first time since she had left twenty-six years previously. She looked serene, unfazed by the chaos around her, perhaps just being reminded. Our destination was the home of my mum's sister, where we would be staying for the next six weeks. My cousin Julian greeted us at the door and asked us if we would like something to drink. Two glasses of guava juice on a tray appeared. This was the beginning of a fascinating voyage of discovery in the homeland of my mother.

I often weave curried foods into the menus at my restaurant. I do this partly in homage to my mother and partly because I am interested in the influences from this part of the world on my interpretation of cooking in general.

Ingredients

5 sweet potatoes
⅓ cup (75 mL) sunflower oil
1 teaspoon (5 mL) ground cumin
1 teaspoon (5 mL) ground coriander
½ teaspoon (2 mL) ground fenugreek
½ teaspoon (2 mL) turmeric
1 tablespoon (15 mL) finely chopped peeled
    fresh ginger
2 cloves garlic, finely minced
2 small green chilies
2 medium onions, finely chopped
12 cups (3 L) vegetable stock
½ cup (125 mL) yogurt
1 cucumber, peeled, seeded and grated
1 teaspoon (5 mL) finely chopped fresh mint
Salt

Directions

Preheat the oven to 350°F (180°C). Place the sweet potatoes on a baking sheet and bake for about 1 hour or until they are soft to the touch. Let cool.

Meanwhile, pour the oil into a large soup pot and place over medium heat. Add the cumin, coriander, fenugreek and turmeric; stir until the spices start to release their heady aromas, approximately 10 minutes.

Add the ginger, garlic, chilies and onions and continue cooking, stirring from time to time, until the onions are translucent, approximately 15 minutes. Add the vegetable stock.

Peel the sweet potatoes and stir the flesh into the stock mixture. Bring to the boil, then reduce heat and simmer for 10 minutes.

Working in batches, transfer the soup to a blender or food processor and blend until smooth. Pour soup back into the pot and gently reheat.

Meanwhile, prepare the raita. In a small bowl, mix together the yogurt, cucumber and mint. Season with salt.

Ladle the soup into 6 bowls. Add a dollop of raita to each bowl and serve.

Niçoise-Style Salad with Albacore Tuna

Makes 4 servings

Giving classic French dishes a new regional Canadian flavour is something that has interested me for many years. Salade niçoise is a beautiful creation, full of sunny reminders of the south of France, where it originated in the sun-drenched city of Nice. I think it is usually a bad idea to take a dish that we enjoyed in its place of origin and recreate it in a new place in the hopes of reliving that wonderful moment, but this salad might be an exception. I use albacore tuna caught off the shores of British Columbia, along with vegetables grown on my farm in Prince Edward County. They combine to make a perfect summer lunch.

Ingredients

4 fresh albacore tuna fillets (3 ounces/90 g each)
A generous sprinkling of salt
¾ cup (175 mL) sunflower oil
1 head of butter lettuce
3½ ounces (100 g) fresh green and yellow beans, trimmed
4 new potatoes
4 small field tomatoes
Salt and freshly ground black pepper
2 shallots, finely chopped
2 tablespoons (30 mL) white wine vinegar
1 small red onion, sliced into thin rounds
20 niçoise-style olives
4 hard-boiled eggs, quartered
4 fresh basil leaves, thinly sliced
¼ cup (60 mL) fine olive oil

Directions

Salt the tuna fillets on both sides and allow them to rest for 1 hour at room temperature.

Heat the sunflower oil in a small saucepan to 150°F (65°C). Place the tuna in the oil and poach for about 1 hour or until the fish feels firm but still yields to the touch. Let cool, then refrigerate the tuna in the oil for at least 1 day and up to 5 days.

When ready to serve, drain the tuna. Tear the lettuce into bite-size pieces.

Cook the beans in a pot of boiling water until tender. Remove the beans, refresh under cold water, drain and reserve. Add salt to the water and cook the potatoes until just tender; drain and cut into slices. Cut the tomatoes into quarters and season with salt and pepper. Stir together the shallots and white wine vinegar.

Divide the lettuce among 4 plates. Arrange the prepared vegetables, onion slices, olives and eggs in a pleasing pattern on the plates. Place a fillet of tuna on each salad. Sprinkle each plate with the shallot vinegar mixture and basil. Drizzle the olive oil over each plate. Season with salt and pepper. Serve.

Navarin and Chop of Lamb

Makes 4 servings

This dish is usually associated with spring. There was a time when spring was the only time of year you could get lamb, which is why many people serve it at Easter. I still like to prepare this dish in spring, but the truth is, lamb can be found at any time of year now. I modernized the original version of this recipe by omitting the flour in the sauce. Serve with boiled new potatoes to complete the dish.

Ingredients

1¼ pounds (625 g) lamb shoulder, cut into large
   cubes

2 cups (500 mL) red wine

2 medium onions, chopped

3 medium carrots, chopped

1 small celery root, peeled and chopped

12 black peppercorns, coarsely ground

3 bay leaves

2 sprigs of fresh rosemary

12 juniper berries, crushed

¼ cup (60 mL) sunflower oil

Salt

2 cups (500 mL) strong lamb stock

1 green chili, finely chopped

1 tablespoon (15 mL) chopped fresh mint

1 tablespoon (15 mL) honey

1 teaspoon (5 mL) white wine vinegar

4 lamb chops, trimmed

1 medium carrot, cut into 1-inch (2.5 cm) pieces

8 miniature white turnips (or 2 white turnips cut
   into quarters)

½ cup (125 mL) fresh fava beans, shelled, blanched
   and peeled

½ cup (125 mL) fresh peas

recipe continues . . .

Directions

In a large bowl, combine the cubed lamb shoulder, red wine, onions, carrots, celery root, peppercorns, bay leaves, rosemary and juniper berries. Marinate, refrigerated, for 2 days.

Place a large, heavy flameproof casserole dish over medium heat. Add the sunflower oil. Remove the lamb from the marinade (reserving the marinade) and season with salt. Working with a few pieces at a time, sear on all sides. Reserve on a plate.

Meanwhile, strain the marinade over a small saucepan, reserving the vegetable mixture; slowly bring the marinade to the boil.

When all the lamb is seared, add the strained vegetables to the casserole dish and cook, stirring from time to time, until golden brown. Strain the wine through a fine-mesh strainer into the pot. Cook until the marinade is reduced by half. Add the lamb stock and bring to the boil. Reduce heat to a simmer and add all the seared lamb and any juices that have accumulated. Return to the boil, then reduce heat to a simmer. Cover and gently simmer for about 2 hours or until the lamb is very tender but doesn't fall apart.

Remove the lamb and reserve. Using a slotted spoon or skimmer, remove and discard the vegetables. Return the braising liquid to the boil over medium heat; reduce by half.

Meanwhile, combine the chili, mint, honey and vinegar in a small bowl to make a paste. Smear the paste over the lamb chops. Reserve.

Add the carrot, turnips and cooked lamb pieces to the braising liquid. Simmer for about 15 minutes or until the vegetables are tender. Add the fava beans and peas.

Season the lamb chops with salt and grill them over medium heat for about 2 minutes on each side.

Lay out 4 soup plates. Place a mound of braised lamb and vegetables in the centre of each plate and top with a ladle of jus. Lean a lamb chop against each mound and serve.

Tomatoes and Other Summer Fruits

I have a special fondness for tomatoes, and the ones that grow at Jamie's farm are like jewels; the variety of shapes and colours they display is such a treat to shoot. It's like they are as individual as people. Their sculptural quality and the anticipation of their flavour are inspiring. To compare the taste experience of a ripe, fresh heirloom tomato and a tasteless, out-of-season tomato pretty much tells the whole story. These tomatoes, for me, are symbolic of what good eating is about.

JO DICKINS, ASSISTANT, PHOTOGRAPHER

J.K. Tomato Sauce

Makes twelve 1-quart (1 L) jars

Toronto is a city of neighbourhoods. In addition to the streets, there is this other network of alleys running parallel to the streets, behind the houses. Cab drivers use them as an alternative route. In the late summer I walk down these alleys. Often on the weekends the garage doors are open. I peer inside to see bushels of plum tomatoes ripening on the floor. Looking beyond the garage, I see a family transforming the deep red tomatoes into sauce. Everyone has shown up to make the sauce together. Everyone has a role and each will walk away with their share of this delicious tangible memory of summer.

This sauce is an all-purpose product. It works great, straight from the jar, for making Bloody Marys. Boil it down with chopped onions, oregano and olive oil to make a beautiful pasta sauce.

Ingredients

50 pounds (23 kg) ripe Roma or San Marzano tomatoes
24 cloves garlic, finely minced
2 tablespoons (30 mL) fine sea salt
1 teaspoon (5 mL) coarsely ground black pepper
60 fresh basil leaves

Directions

For canning instructions, see pages 282–83.

Roughly chop tomatoes or pass them through a tomato milling machine or food mill. In a large pot, bring tomatoes slowly to the boil. Skim the surface. Reduce heat to a simmer and stir in the garlic, salt and pepper. Remove from the heat.

Into each of 12 sterilized 1-quart (1 L) mason jars, place 5 basil leaves, then fill the jars with sauce, leaving ½ inch (1 cm) headspace. Seal jars and process in boiling water for 45 minutes. Cool on the counter and store in a cool, dark place.

133

Iced Tomato Soup

Makes 6 servings

In September 1994 there was a Major League Baseball strike. Around the same time I received a phone call from Robert Lantos and Victor Loewy at Alliance Films. They wanted to know if I was interested in catering their gala party at the museum during the Toronto International Film Festival. At the time I was between restaurants, with nowhere to prepare for a party of five hundred people. Of course I didn't let on, but inside I was sweating bullets. Then I remembered the strike! I had been chef at a dining club in the SkyDome called the Founders Club. I called the manager of the club, a friend, and inquired whether I might be able to use the production kitchen and its staff of cooks during this downtime as a result of the strike. I was happily surprised when he agreed.

It was the beginning of a long relationship between me and Alliance, particularly with Victor and Robert. One hot and humid summer day, Victor came in to J.K. ROM. Nothing on the menu suffered; in his lovable way Victor demanded I make something refreshing for him. I had beautiful tomatoes in my kitchen from a local farmer. I quickly made a soup from these tomatoes with a touch of garlic and basil. I poured the soup through ice cubes to bring the temperature down and served it in an ice bowl. To this day when Victor comes to see me, he will ask for this soup.

Ingredients

6 fresh basil leaves

2 pounds (1 kg) ripe red field tomatoes, cut into pieces

½ clove garlic, finely minced

¼ cup (60 mL) fine olive oil

8 cups (2 L) vegetable stock

Salt and freshly ground black pepper

2 ripe red tomatoes, seeded and finely diced

6 small fresh basil leaves for garnishing

Directions

Chill 6 soup bowls.

In a blender, place 2 of the basil leaves along with one-third each of the tomatoes, garlic, olive oil and stock. Add salt and pepper to taste. Blend at high speed until smooth. Force the mixture through a fine-mesh strainer into a bowl, using a ladle to press on the solids. Repeat the entire process two more times. Mix well and taste for salt.

Place a spoonful of diced tomato in each soup bowl. Pour the soup into the bowls. Garnish with a basil leaf and serve.

Semi-Cured Tomatoes

Makes two 1-quart (1 L) jars

I became very excited to produce semi-cured tomatoes when my friend, farmer Michael Schmidt, gave me construction plans for a solar dehydrator. He had one on his farm, and since it is built on bicycle wheels you can roll it out to where you are harvesting and process the tomatoes straight off the vine. The cultivar of tomato that works best is Principe Borghese. When much of the water has been evaporated, this varietal gives a sweet, balanced flavour.

Ingredients

9 pounds (4 kg) cherry tomatoes
(preferably Principe Borghese)
4 cups (1 L) fine olive oil

Directions

Preheat the oven to 195°F (90°C). Slice each tomato in half lengthwise. Loosely arrange the halves on baking sheets with the cut side facing up. Place in the oven overnight or until most of the water has evaporated but they are not chewy-dry. (Or use a food dehydrator, following the manufacturer's directions.)

Fill two 1-quart (1 L) mason jars with the semi-cured tomatoes. Fill each jar with olive oil. Store in the fridge.

137

Celebration of Tomatoes

Makes 6 servings

In the past twenty years, I've become more and more interested in heritage and heirloom varieties of seeds and cultivars. I've been curious about how gardens were planted before chemical fertilizers and insecticides became available. From my own gardening over the past ten years, I have come to understand that heirloom varieties of tomatoes grow well without using chemical fertilizers or insecticides of any kind.

Ingredients
Dressing
2 egg yolks
1 tablespoon (15 mL) fresh lemon juice
1 teaspoon (5 mL) white wine vinegar
1 teaspoon (5 mL) Dijon mustard
2 tablespoons (30 mL) fresh basil leaves
⅓ cup (75 mL) cold-pressed sunflower oil
Salt and freshly ground black pepper

Celery Root
1 cup (250 mL) sunflower oil
½ cup (125 mL) celery root cut into julienne
Salt

Tomatoes
6 ripe tomatoes of different heirloom varieties
12 cherry tomatoes
Arugula leaves
Salt and freshly ground black pepper

Directions
To make the dressing, in a food processor, add the egg yolks, lemon juice, vinegar and mustard; pulse to combine. Add the basil leaves and process until chopped. While the processor is running, slowly add the sunflower oil. Season with salt and pepper. Reserve.

For the celery root, heat the oil in a small saucepan to 325°F (160°C). Fry the celery root until crispy and golden, about 3 minutes. Remove with a slotted spoon and drain on paper towels. Season with salt. Reserve.

Slice the heirloom tomatoes into thick rounds; cut the cherry tomatoes in half lengthwise. Season with salt and pepper.

Arrange some arugula on the plates. Top with slices of tomato. Drizzle with the dressing and sprinkle over the fried celery root. Finish with salt and freshly ground black pepper. Serve.

Crouton with Fried Green Tomato and Toasted Garlic

Makes 6 servings

Tomatoes love the dog days of August. The intense sun and heat brings the fruit to ripeness. Some years, when there is not so much sun and the weather is a little cooler, chances are that not all the tomatoes on your vine will ripen. Green tomatoes offer a whole other taste experience compared to what a ripe tomato tastes like. They have a savoury complexity that is surprising and delightful.

Ingredients

1 day-old baguette

½ cup (125 mL) olive oil

2 cloves garlic, very thinly sliced

6 slices green tomato

Flaky sea salt

Directions

Preheat the oven to 300°F (150°C). Thinly slice the baguette. Spread the slices on a baking sheet and sprinkle with ¼ cup (60 mL) of the olive oil. Place in the oven and toast until evenly crisp and brown, approximately 20 minutes. Reserve.

Heat the remaining ¼ cup (60 mL) olive oil in a large frying pan over low heat. Add the sliced garlic and slowly fry until evenly golden brown. Remove garlic slices and drain on paper towels. Increase the heat until the oil begins smoking. Add the slices of green tomato and season with salt. Fry, turning once, until golden brown on both sides but still slightly firm.

Cut the fried green tomato to fit on the baguette toasts. Garnish with fried garlic slices. Serve.

Vegetarian Ceviche on Free-Form Potato Crisp

Makes 6 servings

One time in Puerto Vallarta, Mexico, my family and I were sunning ourselves on the beach. A young man pushing a wooden cart painted white was making his way along the beach. His white T-shirt and long white pants matched the paint on the cart. The effect was quite dazzling. He eventually approached us and asked if we would care for any ceviche. He served the most amazing snapper and octopus, mixed with onions, tomatoes and cucumbers, in little plastic cups with Premium brand saltines on the side. Wow! I think two things happened to me there. One was that I realized that excellence in gastronomy could be experienced in other contexts, not just at a white-clothed table. Two, that we needed to improve our street food offerings in Toronto. That ceviche was sublime. I laughed mirthlessly when I thought of the monotonous landscape of hot dog carts littering the streets of Toronto.

Given that the quality of fish available in Toronto could never match the seaside excellence proffered in Mexico, I was inspired to create this delicious vegetarian version of the fish classic.

Ingredients

2 cups (500 mL) sunflower oil
2 medium Yukon Gold potatoes, peeled and
  cut into julienne
Salt
1 tablespoon (15 mL) very finely diced cucumber
1 tablespoon (15 mL) very finely diced peeled
  sweet potato
1 tablespoon (15 mL) very finely chopped red onion
1 tablespoon (15 mL) very finely diced
  seeded tomato
1 tablespoon (15 mL) finely chopped fresh coriander
1 tablespoon (15 mL) fresh lime juice
½ teaspoon (2 mL) finely chopped green chili

Directions

Heat the sunflower oil in a large saucepan to 250°F (120°C). Put the julienned potatoes into the heated oil and cook, stirring continuously, until tender but not browned, about 1 minute. Transfer the potatoes to a baking sheet and let cool slightly. Shape 6 small free-form "nests" with your hands.

Increase the temperature of the oil to 350°F (180°C). Fry the "nests," stirring continuously, until golden brown. Drain on paper towels and sprinkle with salt. Reserve.

In a small bowl, mix the cucumber, sweet potato, red onion, tomato, coriander, lime juice and chili. Season with salt.

Lay out the potato nests on a platter. Spoon the vegetarian ceviche into each nest. Serve.

Hipple Farms, Beamsville, Ontario

Pear and Cheese Melt with Black Currant Purée

Makes 4 servings

Whenever black currants come into season, I always make jam, jelly, purée and juice. Black currants are intensely flavourful in a way that allows them to be served in savoury as well as sweet preparations, as a refreshing dimension to a white wine aperitif, or the counterpoint in this unctuous warm cheese dish.

Ingredients

¾ cup (175 mL) fresh black currants
   (blackberries will work as well)
6 tablespoons (90 mL) honey
¼ cup (60 mL) water
2 just-ripe pears
4 ounces (125 g) local blue cheese, cut into 4 slices

Directions

Preheat the oven to 300°F (150°C).

   Combine the currants, honey and water in a small saucepan. Bring to the boil and cook for approximately 10 minutes, stirring from time to time. Pass the cooked currants through a fine-mesh strainer, pressing on the solids. Reserve the juice.

   Thinly slice the pears crosswise on a mandoline. Use 8 of the larger slices to make 4 sandwiches, with a slice of blue cheese in between. Place the pear and cheese sandwiches on an ungreased baking sheet and warm them in the oven for about 5 minutes or until the cheese begins to run.

   Spoon a small pool of black currant purée onto 4 small plates. Transfer a pear sandwich to each plate. Serve.

147

Peach Melba

Makes 4 servings

I like to make this recipe when Niagara peaches are at their ripest through July and August. However, it can also bring a glimmer of summer to the depths of winter, as it can be prepared using preserved peaches.

Ingredients

½ cup (125 mL) raspberry purée

2 cups (500 mL) vanilla ice cream

4 poached fresh peach halves (or preserved peaches; see recipe page 286)

7 fluid ounces (200 mL) whipping cream, whipped to soft peaks

¼ cup (60 mL) sliced unblanched almonds, toasted until golden brown

Directions

Set out 4 old-fashioned sundae glasses with a pedestal, or martini glasses or bowls. Place about 2 tablespoons (30 mL) of raspberry purée in each glass, 1 large scoop of ice cream on top of the purée and a poached peach half on the ice cream, dome side up. Pipe whipped cream onto each peach Melba. Sprinkle with toasted almonds and serve.

Apricot Jam

Makes six 1-pint (500 mL) jars

These tender little stone fruits grow well in our climate. I use the darker-hued apricots for my jam, which I make with the special addition of one apricot kernel per jar. The apricot is related to the almond, and the kernel lends an interesting marzipan-like quality to the finished jam.

Ingredients

4 pounds (2 kg) firm fresh apricots

4 pounds (2 kg) fine granulated sugar

Directions

For canning instructions, see pages 282–83.

Wash apricots, cut them in half and remove the pits. Crack the pits with a hammer and remove the inner kernel; reserve the kernels.

In a large bowl, mix together the fruit and the sugar. Let macerate overnight, covered, in the refrigerator. The next day, suspend the macerated fruit in a colander over a large pot to collect the syrup.

Bring the syrup to the boil and gently boil until the temperature reaches 220°F (105°C). Add the fruit to the syrup and continue cooking, skimming the surface from time to time, until the temperature again reaches 220°F (105°C).

Remove from the heat and immediately pack 6 sterilized 1-pint (500 mL) mason jars with jam, leaving ¼-inch (5 mm) headspace. Add 1 apricot kernel to each jar. Seal jars and process in boiling water for 15 minutes. Cool on the counter and store in a cool, dark place.

Apricot and Almond Tart

Makes 8 servings

Apricots always suggest something romantic to me. Like the colour in a Dutch masters still life, the colour of the rising sun, all reds and golds. The smell, so perfumed and feminine, the taste, so sweet and deep. They make me think of coffee and cake and jam and reading newspapers in wingback chairs under soft light.

Here in Ontario, we have beautiful apricots. Their season is short, usually around the middle to the end of July. I will go to the Ontario Food Terminal at this time and walk from stall to stall comparing the fruit. I gravitate towards the smaller, smoother-skinned ones with the orangey-red skins and firm texture. I purchase them slightly under-ripe, as I find these give the best results for both baking and preserving.

Ingredients

1 disc (8 ounces/250 g) sweet pastry
   (see recipe page 153)
2 pounds (1 kg) firm fresh apricots,
   halved and pitted
4 eggs
½ cup + 2 tablespoons (125 g) granulated sugar
1 tablespoon (15 mL) vanilla extract
¼ cup (60 g) butter, melted
½ cup (75 g) ground almonds
1 cup + 4 teaspoons (100 g) sifted pastry flour

Directions

Preheat the oven to 350°F (180°C). Lightly grease and flour a 10-inch (25 cm) tart pan with removable bottom.

Roll out pastry into a disc about ⅛ inch (3 mm) thick. Fit it into the pan and trim the edges. Line with parchment paper or foil and fill with baking weights. Bake until theedge is golden, about 30 minutes. Remove parchment and weights and cool on a rack.

Preheat the oven to 350°F (180°C).

Pack the apricots into the tart shell, standing them upright in concentric circles, until you have filled the shell. It is surprising how many apricot halves will fit.

In a heatproof bowl, whisk together the eggs and sugar over a saucepan of boiling water until the mixture feels slightly warm to the touch. Using an electric mixer, beat until light and fluffy, about 5 minutes. Add the vanilla, butter, ground almonds and flour; fold in just until combined. Pour the cake batter over the apricot halves. Give the tart a shake to settle the batter all around the apricot halves.

Bake until golden brown and a tester inserted in the cake comes out clean, approximately 40 minutes. Cool on a rack for 2 hours before serving. Serve with whipped cream and strong coffee.

Sweet Pastry

Makes eight 8-ounce (250 g) discs

Here is a recipe for a quantity of sweet pastry that you can divide into discs and store in your freezer. If you don't have vanilla sugar, use granulated sugar and add 1 teaspoon (5 mL) vanilla extract with the eggs.

Ingredients

10 cups (1 kg) all-purpose flour
Pinch of salt
2½ cups (600 g) cold butter
3 eggs
1¾ cups (325 g) vanilla sugar

Directions

Combine the flour and salt in a large bowl. Cut the butter into ½-inch (1 cm) cubes and blend into flour using both hands or a pastry blender until the mixture resembles coarse meal. Do not over-mix. Whisk the eggs and sugar together. Add to the flour mixture and mix just until combined.

Divide the dough into 8 equal pieces. Shape each piece into a ball and flatten into a disc. Wrap in plastic wrap and freeze in resealable plastic bags for up to 3 months.

153

Golden Plum Upside-Down Cake with Dulce de Leche Ice Cream

Makes 8 servings

Golden plums come onto the market around the middle of July each year. The Niagara region produces wonderful fruit. These sweet plums are great to eat raw but have a complexity that reveals itself best when cooked.

Ingredients

Caramel Topping

¾ cup (190 g) butter, softened

2 cups (400 g) lightly packed brown sugar

3 tablespoons (50 mL) honey

1 teaspoon (5 mL) amber rum

1 teaspoon (5 mL) vanilla extract

Cake

3 cups (285 g) sifted pastry flour

4 teaspoons (20 mL) baking powder

¾ cup (190 g) softened butter

1 cup (200 g) granulated sugar

4 eggs

1 teaspoon (5 mL) vanilla extract

3 tablespoons (50 mL) milk

2 pounds (1 kg) golden plums, halved and pitted

Dulce de leche ice cream for serving

Dircctions

Preheat the oven to 350°F (180°C). Grease and flour the sides of an 8-inch (2 L) springform pan, then grease the bottom.

To make the caramel topping, in a medium bowl, cream the butter with the sugar until light and fluffy. Add the honey, rum and vanilla and mix well. Spread the caramel topping in the bottom of the prepared pan.

To make the cake, sift together the flour and baking powder. In a large bowl, cream the butter with the sugar until light and fluffy. In a separate bowl, whisk together the eggs and vanilla. Gradually beat the eggs into the butter mixture. Beat in the milk. Gradually fold in the flour mixture.

Arrange a layer of closely spaced plum halves, cut side down, over the caramel. Pour the cake batter on top. Bake for about 50 minutes or until a cake tester comes out clean. Cool on a rack for 30 minutes before inverting onto a cake plate. Cool an additional 30 minutes before serving.

Serve with a dollop of dulce de leche ice cream.

155

Weathering the Storm

Things were chugging along nicely at J.K. ROM. The restaurant was going very well. I had been building my business for nine years and I was at the point where the business was profitable. Then, in 2002, the museum served me notice. They said that on April 30, 2003, my lease would be over. So I had some planning to do. At that time the company employed about forty people. I had a lunch operation and an events-based dinner operation at J.K. ROM and in the museum in general.

When J.K. ROM closed its doors most of the staff were laid off. With my core staff, we kept the catering going, but we all agreed that we needed a downtown location for the business. I was convinced that the best model for a business in Toronto was an event venue because I knew that the margins on events were higher than with an à la carte restaurant. With that as our focus we started looking for a location downtown. We found it at 9 Church Street. It was a wonderful space, and we felt we could transpose what we had been doing at the ROM into the venue without too much trouble.

The one problem was that event spaces are essentially closed to the public, and I have always had the idea that it was important to be accessible. That's really been a founding principle of Jamie Kennedy Kitchens. Out of that thinking came the Wine Bar. We developed a little space that would allow people to come in and have something simple. The idea was to serve small plates of food with an intelligently chosen, comprehensive wine list to go along with them.

So Jamie Kennedy Wine Bar opened. We were not prepared for what an instant success it was. It struck a chord with diners in Toronto. It was a style that people wanted and were looking for, but nobody had really presented it until then. The Wine Bar captured the zeitgeist, and people came in droves. We received a lot of positive notice in the press.

Now I realize that just about every major trend that would blow through Toronto in the early 2000s was already encapsulated in the Wine Bar. Small plates. Reasonable prices. Deliberately casual ambience. Do-it-yourself charcuterie and preserves. Very serious cheeses.

JAMES CHATTO, FOOD WRITER

Gradually, the catering took a back seat and the Wine Bar became the main focus for Jamie Kennedy Kitchens. We were feeling optimistic, and invincible. Let's expand!

We had had, with the ROM, an association with a cultural institution. So we thought we should do it again. That's what brought us to the Gardiner Museum. Being the exclusive caterer for the Gardiner meant we'd have a much-increased schedule of catering events. We realized that we needed more space, a commissary kitchen to do prep and production work for catering as well as for the Wine Bar. We needed to expand beyond 9 Church Street to a space where we could actually get the production work done in order to fulfill that new event business and still maintain the à la carte operation at the Wine Bar. The kitchen at the Wine Bar was bursting. It was already very stressed just trying to produce the food we were serving there, never mind being able to handle a much-increased number of catering events.

Riding this wave of optimism about our company, we took on the Gardiner in 2006 and rented the space that became Gilead. We did a total renovation of Gilead in order to have a complete kitchen and a little café. Gilead was essentially a catering kitchen, but the café kept it consistent with our philosophy of having public access. At that point we were operating J.K. at the Gardiner, Gilead Café and the J.K. Wine Bar, plus we were working towards capacity in our catering calendar.

As an entrepreneur you have times of strength and times of weakness. I think there were many issues that contributed to what happened in 2008/2009, but the bottom line was that I was facing the near collapse of the entire company because we were simply overextended, and the economic downturn didn't help things either. I needed to look very closely at what was going on in the business and weigh all our options, then decide how to proceed.

I got advice from an insolvency expert. He was advising me on how to emerge from a potential bankruptcy with maybe my personal possessions still intact. There was a lot of that kind of counsel going on. All I could think was "Are you kidding? This doesn't make any sense. Why are we failing so badly? We have a great product, a great brand. This is crazy." I said to him, "Please give me some advice on how we may remain whole—how the company can stay whole and fight its way through this downturn."

What we did had few precedents in the province of Ontario, but I was able to do it because the Wine Bar, as part of my business, was quantifiable. It was a piece of the company that I could sell. By selling it I sent the message to my creditors that I wasn't giving up. It would have been much easier to just declare bankruptcy.

Instead I set about the work of restructuring what was left of my company. We re-established our core of business at Gilead and continued to build our catering calendar. When you go through a crisis like that, you just become a survivor and you build up your business again. That's been the work of the last five years and it continues today.

I don't give up casily.

159

I haven't always been as patient or as diligent as my dad, but seeing his dedication to quality that never wavers definitely inspires me. In the face of defeat his perseverance is incredible, he just keeps on going and always finds a way to make it work. I remember we were at an event once and we didn't have enough oil for the fryer, so he sent me to gather some rocks. We cleaned them and dropped them in to raise the level of the oil in the fryer. He's shown me how to work my way out of a tight spot so many times.

MICHA KENNEDY, SON

Communal Table

The Communal Table Dinner at Evergreen Brick Works on June 19, 2010, was intended in part to raise a decent profit with which to pay down some outstanding balances with patient and understanding suppliers. With no budget for table decor, Jamie liked my idea of Russian olive boughs interspersed with the colourful jars of preserves from Gilead. During the meal I noticed that many guests had opened jars to eat the contents. Jodi McBurney (Jamie's manager at the time) and I were panicking, but Jamie was completely cool about it. It was a costly but humorous moment in an unforgettable evening.

JO DICKINS, ASSISTANT, PHOTOGRAPHER

Opposite, upper left: Evergreen's Geoff Cape greets guests. *Opposite, lower right*: Chef Dan DeMatteis.
This page, lower left: Artist Tom Dean and Chef Brad Long

Great Lakes Chowder

Makes 6 servings

This soup takes the bounty of our Great Lakes and channels it into a classic New England chowder recipe. The only thing missing might be those little packages of oyster crackers that you get in New England diners.

Ingredients

Fumet (stock)

4 pounds (2 kg) pickerel or whitefish bones

Bouquet garni of thinly sliced onions, leeks, celery root and fennel, coarsely ground black pepper, bay leaf

4 cups (1 L) water

2 cups (500 mL) white wine

Chowder Base

6 tablespoons (100 g) butter

2 ounces (60 g) smoked bacon, diced

2 medium onions, finely chopped

2 celery stalks, diced

1 leek, diced

1 fennel bulb, diced

2 medium Yukon Gold potatoes, peeled and diced

2 bay leaves

2 whole cloves

12 black peppercorns, crushed

Great Lakes Fish

⅔ cup (150 g) butter

1 cup (250 mL) white wine

2 shallots, finely chopped

Salt

6 ounces (180 g) fresh skinless pickerel fillet, cut into medium pieces

6 ounces (180 g) fresh skinless whitefish fillet, cut into medium pieces

6 ounces (180 g) fresh skinless yellow perch fillets, cut in half on the bias

3 tablespoons (50 mL) chopped fresh parsley

Directions

To make the fumet, simmer the fish bones, bouquet garni, water and wine in a medium saucepan for 30 minutes, loosely covered. Strain through a fine-mesh strainer. Reserve.

To make the chowder base, in a stock pot, melt the butter over low heat. Add the bacon, onions, celery, leek, fennel, potatoes, bay leaves, cloves and peppercorns. Sweat the ingredients, without caramelizing, for 20 minutes, stirring regularly with a wooden spoon. Add the fumet and bring to the boil over high heat. Reduce heat and simmer for 5 minutes.

Remove half of the vegetables and reserve. Discard bay leaves. Purée the contents of the stock pot in a blender. Wipe out the pot and force the puréed chowder base through a fine-mesh strainer back into the pot.

For the Great Lakes Fish, in a large saucepan, combine the butter, wine and shallots. Bring to the boil. Add salt to taste. Reduce heat to a simmer. Add all the fish at once and gently poach until just cooked through, about 5 minutes.

Lay out 6 soup bowls and divide the poached fish equally among them. Add the reserved diced vegetables to the bowls.

Add the poaching liquid to the chowder base. Bring to the boil. Ladle over the fish and vegetables. Garnish with chopped parsley and serve.

Barbecued and Grilled Cumbrae's Beef

Makes 6 servings

Stephen Alexander owns Cumbrae Farms. One day he took me on a tour of the farms he contracts to raise beef cattle for his butcher shops. He was so passionate as he described the protocols he has developed to raise cattle in a way that provides his customers with superior locally and ethically raised beef. I support people like Stephen because I see that their dedication to good food mirrors my own.

Ingredients

1 teaspoon (5 mL) each salt, granulated sugar and
    sweet Spanish paprika
¼ teaspoon (1 mL) chili flakes
6 beef short ribs, cut into 2-inch (5 cm) lengths
    (1¼ pounds/625 g)
2 tablespoons (30 mL) sunflower oil, plus extra for
    rubbing onto steaks
4 cups (1 L) beef stock
2 rib steaks (10 ounces/300 g each)
Salt and freshly ground black pepper

BBQ Sauce
⅔ cup (150 mL) sunflower oil
2 pounds (1 kg) onions, finely chopped
5 cloves garlic, finely chopped
1 tablespoon (15 mL) chopped peeled fresh ginger
2 apples (any kind), peeled, cored and chopped
2 celery stalks, chopped
6 jalapeño peppers, thinly sliced
Salt and freshly ground black pepper
5 pounds (2.2 kg) ripe Roma tomatoes, roughly
    chopped
½ cup (125 mL) honey
½ cup (125 mL) cider vinegar

Directions

In a small bowl, stir together the salt, sugar, paprika and chili flakes. Rub the dry rub mixture onto the short ribs. Cover and refrigerate for 24 hours.

In a frying pan, heat the sunflower oil. Sear the short ribs until deep brown on all sides.

Bring the beef stock to the boil in a large pot and add the seared short ribs. Reduce heat to a simmer, cover and braise until the bone comes easily away from the meat, approximately 2 hours. Reserve, keeping warm.

Meanwhile, make the BBQ sauce. In a large soup pot, heat the sunflower oil over low heat. Add the onions, garlic, ginger, apples, celery, jalapeño peppers, and salt and pepper to taste; gently sauté for approximately 15 minutes. When everything is soft and translucent, add the tomatoes, honey and cider vinegar. Bring to the boil, then reduce heat, cover and simmer for 2 hours, stirring from time to time.

Purée sauce in a food processor and strain through a fine-mesh strainer. Return to the pot and keep warm.

Preheat grill. I like to use a charcoal barbecue with natural charcoal. Season steaks with salt and pepper. Rub with some sunflower oil. Grill steaks to desired doneness, turning only once. Let steaks relax on a cutting board for 10 minutes.

Lay out 6 plates. Place a short rib on each plate. Nap with BBQ sauce. Carve steaks across the grain into thick slices. Arrange slices on each plate. Serve with a baked potato and salad.

fall

THE WALLS AT GILEAD CAFÉ FILL UP AGAIN WITH

MULTICOLOURED MASON JARS OF PICKLED BEETS,

ROASTED PEPPERS, JAMS AND DILL PICKLES.

THEY CREATE A BACKDROP TO OUR RESTAURANT

THAT IS BOTH FORM AND FUNCTION.

Matt Caudle and Robert Cram of Heretical Objects
installed their work "Dirt" at Pleasant Valley Farm in 2013.

Jamie's Vineyard: Weeds vs. Vines

Most vineyards are producing grapes within two years of starting up. Mine took nine. I had my first harvest in 2011. I'm a cook, not a winemaker. I went out and planted vines before I even knew anything about farming. I was completely seduced by the romantic notion of making wine on my property. It was something I wanted to do, so I just went ahead and did it. My neighbour Geoff Heinricks is a writer and winegrower who wrote a book about his experience starting a vineyard in the county called *A Fool and Forty Acres*. He coached me through the process of planting my vines by hand. There was a lot of information about tending the vines that he taught me. But I could only absorb so much. I'm an experiential and tactile learner—I understood the theory, but I needed to do it in practice.

There were a few things that were going against me, but primarily it was my ignorance of farming. I did not realize that when you clear a field of brush, you are igniting the germination of thousands of weed seeds that had been lying dormant. I planted the vines but I didn't bargain for the weeds. The weeds won against the vines for the first six years. The vines didn't die because of the weeds, but they didn't thrive. They were almost bonsai. They were there and they would grow, but they never bore fruit, the flowers never got pollinated because they were just buried in this morass of weeds. Being the weekend weed warrior just wasn't enough.

That was another thing I learned about vineyards: during the growing season they require daily attention. There are very few days when you can just leave them alone. In year five or six I hired two agricultural workers to help me bring the vineyard up to a level where it could actually produce fruit. That meant getting rid of the weeds, creating nice beds for the vines, burying canes. Then I started seeing the buds. They looked like tiny little bunches of grapes, on the end of the stem in amongst all the leaves. What a feeling to finally start seeing them! I'd only seen them in pictures in books or on other people's vines, never on my own. It was amazing.

We planted Jamie's vineyard on a bluff, very steep with beautiful southern exposure.
There's a fair number of these bluffs out here in the County, mostly ignored because they're hard to
work. The southern slope gets the beautiful breeze from the lake, and the land holds the heat. If you
know anything about microclimates and soils, you know right away that this is a good spot.
Shallow limestone soil like this is very rare in North America.

I plant by hand, and that hill is too steep for machinery. When it came time to plant Jamie's vines
I'd already dug thousands of holes in my life. I'd dig and plant three or four in the time it took him
to do one. I remember Jamie saying, "It's not fair." I just said, "If we were in the kitchen and I'm
still cutting my first onion when you've done all your mise en place, *I'd be saying the same thing."*

GEOFF HEINRICKS, WINEMAKER AND AUTHOR

Jamie's whole approach is that he's capturing the essence of Ontario, not only the great products
but the spirit of the people behind them. He's one of the leaders in supporting Ontario wine.
This is a novelty for Ontario. For a long time our wine lists were dominated by foreign wines,
whereas if you go to Burgundy, all the wine lists are Burgundian, because the wines
of the region work with the food of the region.

Jamie knows that the wines of Ontario belong with the food that has been grown and made here.

NORMAN HARDIE, WINEMAKER, MEMBER OF THE SOMEWHERENESS GROUP

ONTARIO WINE THEN AND NOW

When I started in my restaurant career in 1974, Ontario had a fledgling wine industry. Growers wisely made the decision to pull out most of the *Vitis labrusca* grapes that are native to the region and replace them with *Vitis vinifera*, the European grapevines that produce lovely table wines like Chardonnay and Pinot Noir.

John Marynissen, Paul Bosc, Donald Ziraldo and Karl Kaiser were early experimenters. Somewhere along the line there was an understanding that European varietals could work in our climate and in Niagara specifically. The mesoclimate—the topographic influence on a vineyard's climate, such as the hills and valleys, the distance from water and so on—allows grapes to come to ripeness before frost, and there are more frost-free days in Niagara than in any other part of Ontario, with the exception of maybe Pelee Island. This was great news for grape growers; it was a catalyst for the revolution of the wine industry in Ontario. Labrusca grapes out, European varietals in.

Now that I've experienced the planting and the pruning, the growing and the harvesting, I can observe with a keener eye the actions of my neighbours—Norm Hardie; Geoff; my friends at the Old Third, Bruno and Jens; Long Dog Winery; Redtail Vineyard; Closson Chase. These are people who are interested in producing small-quantity handcrafted wines.

Back in the '70s my interest in food from this province was in step with the interest in wine in this province. It's been a steady rise in awareness, in quality and in price point. All these things mark something that is economically and culturally successful. These are exciting times.

Ajo Blanco with Pinot Noir Grapes and Jeff's Sunflower Oil

Makes 6 servings

My love affair with Spain began in December 1977. I had travelled to Seville to surprise my friend Peter, who was taking his third year of school abroad at the university there. I had journeyed from Paris, where there was a general strike in effect, of course, shutting down all public services. I walked to the outskirts of town and hitch-hiked to Barcelona. There I boarded a train and travelled a further twelve hours by rail to reach my destination. During that train ride I tasted *jamón* for the first time. But that is another story. Paris had been cold and grey and, believe it or not, I was depressed. When I arrived in Seville, I felt so much better. I felt an affinity for the place, the people, the culture, like I had never felt before or since. I'm surprised I ever left.

This recipe is inspired by a classic cold soup from La Mancha called *ajo blanco*. My friend and colleague Adolfo Muñoz prepared this soup when he came to visit me in Toronto. I was amazed by the depth of flavour and complexity from so few ingredients. My adaptation of that soup celebrates some local flavours.

Ingredients

2 cups (250 g) whole unpeeled almonds
3 slices white bread, crusts removed
1⅔ cups (400 mL) water
3 cloves garlic, thinly sliced
⅓ cup (75 mL) cider vinegar
6 tablespoons (90 mL) cold-pressed sunflower oil, plus extra for drizzling
Salt
9 fresh Pinot Noir grapes or local seedless grapes
12 to 18 small croutons

Directions

Bring a large saucepan of water to the boil. Add the almonds, bring back to the boil, and boil for 3 minutes. Drain almonds. When they are cool enough to handle, pop the skins off. Discard skins.

Cut the bread into rough pieces and place in a bowl. Add the water and soak for 10 minutes. Transfer the water and bread to a blender and blend to combine. Add the garlic slices and blend until smooth. Add the almonds and blend until smooth. Add the cider vinegar and blend just to combine. While the blender is running, slowly add the sunflower oil. Season with salt. Transfer soup to a pitcher and refrigerate for 2 hours.

Chill 6 soup bowls in the fridge or freezer for 30 minutes.

Slice the grapes in half. Pour the chilled soup into the bowls. Carefully place 3 grape halves on the surface of each serving. Drizzle some sunflower oil on the surface. Garnish each serving with 2 or 3 croutons. Serve.

Coq au Baco

Makes 4 servings

I have always been a big fan of coq au vin. Clearly, this is a French dish in origin. Part of my creative process is to give a local twist to classic French dishes. The wine plays an important role in the preparation of coq au vin, and I have taken the delicate flavour of the Burgundy wine—the wine of the region of France this dish hails from—and transposed the original idea onto the vineyards of Ontario, where some wineries have made a real success of producing a red wine from the hybrid varietal Baco Noir. The grape produces wines with a deep colour and complex flavour profile.

Ingredients

1 chicken (3 to 4 pounds/1.5 to 2 kg),
    cut into 8 pieces

2 medium onions, roughly chopped

1 carrot, scrubbed and roughly chopped

2 celery stalks, roughly chopped

2 cloves garlic, thinly sliced

12 black peppercorns, cracked

1 small bunch of fresh thyme

2 bay leaves

1 bottle (750 mL) Ontario Baco Noir

½ cup (125 mL) sunflower oil

¼ cup (60 mL) tomato paste

Salt and freshly ground black pepper

2 cups (500 mL) chicken stock

12 small new potatoes

A 3-ounce (90 g) piece of bacon, cut into lardons
    (thick rectangles)

12 pearl onions, peeled

12 firm white mushrooms, cut into quarters
    lengthwise

1 carrot, cut into rectangles

1 leek, cut into thin strips

1 tablespoon (15 mL) chopped fresh parsley

Directions

Place the chicken, onions, carrot, celery, garlic, peppercorns, thyme, bay leaves and wine in a stainless steel bowl. Cover with a plate and marinate for 2 days in the refrigerator, turning the pieces of chicken from time to time.

Preheat the oven to 400°F (200°C).

Place a colander over a large saucepan and strain the chicken and vegetables. Reserve the wine in the saucepan. Remove the chicken pieces and reserve.

Spread the vegetables in a roasting pan and sprinkle with ¼ cup (60 mL) of the sunflower oil. Roast for 10 minutes. Stir in the tomato paste and continue roasting until vegetables are deeply coloured but not burnt, 15 to 20 minutes.

Meanwhile, over low heat, slowly bring the wine to the boil. Place the remaining ¼ cup (60 mL) sunflower oil in a large frying pan over medium heat. Season the chicken pieces on all sides with salt and pepper. Gently fry the chicken until golden brown on all sides. Remove chicken and reserve.

Discard the oil from the frying pan. When the wine starts to boil, return the frying pan to medium heat. Strain the wine through a fine-mesh strainer into the frying pan.

Remove the nicely roasted vegetables from the oven and place the roasting pan on the stove. Add the wine and the chicken stock. Bring to the boil. Add the chicken pieces, cover and return the pan to the oven. Reduce oven temperature to 300°F (150°C) and braise for about 1 hour.

About 30 minutes before the chicken is ready, boil the new potatoes in a pot of salted water until tender; drain and reserve, keeping warm. While the potatoes are cooking, gently sauté the bacon lardons in a frying pan until they render some fat into the pan. Add the pearl onions, mushrooms, carrot and leek. Gently sauté for about 20 minutes or until the vegetables are tender.

Lay out 4 large dinner plates or soup plates. Divide the chicken equally among the plates. Place 3 potatoes on each plate. Spoon the vegetables and bacon equally onto each plate. Strain the braising liquid through a fine-mesh strainer, discarding the solids, and spoon some of the braising liquid over each plate. Sprinkle with parsley and serve.

Vine Cuttings Beef

Makes 4 servings

Through observation, I am beginning to understand the annual cycle of my vineyard. If the winter has been kind, exposed canes containing fruiting buds that were formed last year will have survived. On each vine there is one cane that we lay down in fall and cover with earth to protect it from severe frost during the winter months. It is a form of crop insurance. In mid-April we uncover the cane, redistribute the earth and assess the architecture of each vine. Some rather severe pruning takes place at this juncture. It is these prunings that fuel the fire for this experiment in terroir-based gastronomy.

The cows graze all around the vineyard. Each year I butcher four animals. The cows eat grass and hay only, so the taste of the meat reflects the sweet meadow of mixed grasses where they pasture. I cook the meat over the vine cuttings and serve it with my own wine, everything from the same place creating a delicious harmony at the table.

Ingredients

4 cloves garlic, finely minced

1 tablespoon (15 mL) finely chopped dried
    ancho chili

1 tablespoon (15 mL) sweet Spanish paprika

1 tablespoon (15 mL) coarsely ground black pepper

1 tablespoon (15 mL) chopped fresh parsley

1 teaspoon (5 mL) fresh thyme leaves

3 tablespoons (50 mL) sunflower oil

4 rib-eye steaks (6 ounces/180 g each)

Salt

Directions

In a charcoal barbecue, make a fire using vine cuttings. If no vine cuttings are available, use charcoal instead. While the fire is burning down, mix the garlic, ancho chili, paprika, black pepper, parsley, thyme and oil to make a paste. Rub the paste over both sides of the steaks. Sprinkle the steaks with salt.

When the fire has burnt down to embers, grill the steaks for approximately 8 minutes on each side for medium. Adjust cooking time based on personal preference.

Serve with a local Pinot Noir and your favourite vegetable accompaniments.

Beef and Pork

Raising Beef

I've been cooking for almost forty years and only in the last fifteen to twenty years have I started to question how my meat is being raised and slaughtered. What I discovered is not a pretty picture. Beef cattle are slaughtered at eighteen months; that is considered the optimum moment, as the animals are fully grown and in prime condition. If they are kept alive any longer, there is a diminishing return on investment. So the raising, and the slaughtering, of beef is based entirely on a pretty cold economic calculation. What is lost in the calculation, of course, is not only any consideration for animal welfare but also taste. The longer you keep an animal alive, the more the flavour develops. It doesn't make the meat any tougher or anything like that, and if I served it to your great-grandfather he would recognize that flavour as beef. These days, our beef tastes nothing like what it would have back then.

I like to experiment with things myself, so I raised cattle on my farm for a few years. I wanted to raise beef to three years of age. This was a protocol I had learned from Bill Niman of Niman Ranch. Niman developed a set of beef cattle protocols in the U.S. that essentially ensures the quality of beef for the consumer. So whether you are raising beef in Wyoming or North Dakota, if you are following his protocols, your beef is basically Niman approved and therefore of the highest quality—a sort of haute couture version of beef. Chefs went crazy for it. Stephen Alexander of Cumbrae Farms has applied similar protocols for his own farm in Ontario and the other farms that supply his butcher shops. Anyway, I bought sixteen head of an old breed called Linebacks: four cows and twelve steers. I got four calves a year, and I slaughtered four steers each year, so the herd remained constant at around sixteen. The beef I grew kept my restaurant supplied four months of the year. The rest of the year I purchased from Cumbrae Farms.

Tartare on Crisp Brioche Rounds

Makes 12 canapés

The preparation of this dish was allegedly inspired by nomadic hunters (Tartars) who travelled the countryside of Russia on horseback. They hunted, and while on the move, would put pieces of meat between their saddle and the horse. After riding all day, they would sit down to a meal of pre-salted game. This story may or may not be true. This version is slightly more evolved and can be prepared easily in your own kitchen.

Ingredients

1 brioche loaf

6 ounces (180 g) local hormone- and
   antibiotic-free beef tenderloin,
   finely chopped (1 cup/250 mL)

2 egg yolks

1 medium shallot, very finely chopped

2 tablespoons (30 mL) fine olive oil

1 tablespoon (15 mL) finely chopped fresh parsley

1 tablespoon (15 mL) finely chopped fresh thyme

1 tablespoon (15 mL) Dijon mustard

1 tablespoon (15 mL) tomato paste or
   homemade ketchup

1 tablespoon (15 mL) cognac

1 teaspoon (5 mL) capers, chopped

Pinch of freshly grated nutmeg

Salt and freshly ground black pepper

Directions

Preheat the oven to 300°F (150°C). Cut a few ¼-inch (5 mm) slices from the brioche. Using a 2-inch (5 cm) cookie cutter, cut out rounds. Slice more brioche if needed until you have 12 rounds. Lay them on a baking sheet and toast them in the oven. Reserve.

Just before serving, in a medium bowl, combine the beef, egg yolks, shallot, olive oil, parsley, thyme, mustard, tomato paste, cognac, capers and nutmeg. Mix well. Season with salt and pepper.

Portion the beef mixture into 12 balls and place on the toasted brioche rounds. You can make these look tidier by doing this: using the flat side of a knife, gently press each ball down to form a patty. Using the sharp edge of the knife, score the patty in a grid pattern. Serve.

Braised Oxtail with Marrow Toast

Makes 6 servings

This dish was on the menu at the J.K. Wine Bar when we first opened. There were customers who came in specifically to have it. Our sommelier, Jamie Drummond, would make some genius wine pairing and people would sit sipping their wine patiently waiting for the dish to be set in front of them. Oxtail is one of those unsung heroes that I like to bring into the light once in a while. At Taste, an annual event in Prince Edward County featuring the foods and wines of the region, I prepared a poutine using oxtail and a five-year-old local cheddar from Black River Cheese Company. I cooked at this event for many years, and each year I had a lineup for that poutine that never dwindled until the day was over. Prepared with patience and love, oxtail is a beautiful thing.

Ingredients

4 pounds (2 kg) oxtail, cut into 2-inch (5 cm) pieces

2 medium carrots, cut into large dice

2 medium onions, cut into large dice

1 celery root, peeled and cut into large dice

3 cloves garlic, sliced

12 black peppercorns, coarsely ground

1 small sprig of fresh thyme

3 bay leaves

2 cups (500 mL) red wine

Salt and freshly ground black pepper

4 tablespoons (60 mL) sunflower oil

6 tablespoons (90 mL) tomato paste

2 cups (500 mL) strong beef stock

12 slices of bread, cut into rectangles about 1 × 2 inches (2.5 × 5 cm)

1 carrot, cut into ¼-inch (5 mm) dice

2 leeks, cut into ¼-inch (5 mm) dice

1 celery root, peeled and cut into ¼-inch (5 mm) dice

2 pounds (1 kg) centre-cut beef shank bones, cut about 1 inch (2.5 cm) long (ask your butcher to cut the bones for you)

Flaky sea salt

Directions

Place the oxtail, the large-diced carrots, onions and celery root, garlic, peppercorns, thyme, bay leaves and wine in a large bowl or lidded container. Cover and refrigerate for 48 hours.

Preheat the oven to 375°F (190°C). Remove the oxtail from the marinade and season liberally with salt and pepper. In a large frying pan, heat 2 tablespoons (30 mL) of the oil and sear oxtail on all sides until golden brown. Transfer to a roasting pan.

Strain the marinade, reserving the wine in a small saucepan. Transfer the vegetable mixture to the roasting pan and sprinkle with the remaining 2 tablespoons (30 mL) sunflower oil. Roast until golden brown, stirring from time to time, about 30 minutes. Stir in the tomato paste and continue to roast until the paste has darkened substantially and clings to the vegetables, 15 more minutes. Remove from the oven and reduce oven temperature to 300°F (150°C).

Meanwhile, heat the wine over low heat.

Place the roasting pan over medium heat. Strain the wine through a fine-mesh strainer over the oxtail and vegetables; boil until reduced by approximately half. Add the beef stock, cover and simmer for approximately 3 hours or until the meat easily pulls away from the bone.

Remove the oxtail to a plate. Strain the braising liquid through a fine-mesh strainer into a large saucepan. Discard the vegetables. Reduce the braising liquid by three-quarters.

Meanwhile, lay out the bread rectangles on a baking sheet and toast in the oven until golden brown. Reserve. Increase oven temperature to 325°F (160°C).

Pull all the meat from the oxtail bones. Add the meat and the small-diced carrot, leeks and celery root to the reduced braising liquid. Simmer for 5 minutes.

Meanwhile, carefully push the marrow from the shank bones. Slice the marrow into 24 thick coins using a sharp knife, dipping the knife in hot water before each slice. Place 2 overlapping slices of marrow on each toast. Place toasts on a baking sheet and heat in the oven until the marrow begins to melt, about 5 minutes.

Spoon the oxtail mixture into 6 warm bowls. Float 2 marrow toasts on top of each bowl. Sprinkle sea salt onto the marrow on each toast. Serve.

Pork and Beans

Makes 8 servings

I think of a time long ago when a dish like this would help people get through the harsh Ontario winters, not only with its hearty, filling warmth but also in its preparation, which requires a lot of low and slow cooking, which makes the meal but also warms the house.

Ingredients

1 pound (500 g) dried navy beans, soaked overnight

3 onions (1 cut in half lengthwise and 2 finely chopped)

2 carrots, cut in half lengthwise

2 celery stalks, cut into 4-inch (10 cm) pieces

10 cloves garlic (6 cut in half lengthwise and 4 minced)

2 bay leaves

10 black peppercorns

3½ ounces (100 g) smoked bacon, cut into lardons (thick rectangles)

3½ ounces (100 g) confit pork belly (see recipe page 198), cut into lardons (thick rectangles)

4 cups (1 L) tomato purée

8 cups (2 L) chicken stock

⅔ cup (150 mL) maple syrup

½ cup (125 mL) molasses

Salt and freshly ground black pepper

Directions

Drain the beans and put them in a large pot together with the onion halves, carrots, celery, garlic halves, bay leaves and peppercorns. Cover with water. Bring to the boil, then reduce heat and simmer, uncovered, for 2 hours.

Meanwhile, in a large, heavy pot or Dutch oven, gently sauté the smoked bacon and confit pork belly for 5 minutes. Add the finely chopped onions and the minced garlic; continue to gently sauté for an additional 10 minutes.

Add the tomato purée and continue to cook, stirring regularly, until most of the water has evaporated from the tomatoes, approximately 15 minutes.

Add the chicken stock, maple syrup and molasses. Bring to the boil, then reduce heat and simmer for 15 minutes.

Drain the beans, discarding the vegetables and bay leaves. Stir the beans into the sauce, cover and simmer for an additional 2 hours or until the beans are tender. Season with salt and pepper.

J.K. Burgers

Makes 12 burgers

I remember celebrating fall weekends with family and friends at Wilket Creek Park in Don Mills. We would go early to secure one of those Parks and Rec standard-issue swivelling charcoal barbecues. I would bring along a bag of natural lump maple wood charcoal and fire up the barbecue. In the cooler, a tray stacked with burgers. Everyone seated around a couple of picnic tables pushed together, eating burgers and drinking beer. Hamburgers always taste better when grilled over charcoal.

At Jamie Kennedy Kitchens we use an adaptation of an English muffin for our bun that was developed by the incomparable Rachelle Cadwell, a baker and pastry chef who once worked at Jamie Kennedy Kitchens but is now a restaurateur in her own right, with her husband, Chef Scott Vivian. But some people like the ubiquitous good old spongy sweet white-bread bun for their burger. To each his own. For accompaniments I go with mayonnaise, dill pickles, lettuce, onion, sliced tomatoes in season and Kozlik's Dijon mustard.

Ask your butcher to mix in about 20 percent fat to the total volume of ground meat. This helps to make a juicy burger.

Ingredients

3¾ pounds (1.8 kg) ground chuck or blade steak
3 eggs
2 onions, finely chopped
¼ cup (60 mL) Dijon mustard
¼ cup (60 mL) Worcestershire sauce
3 tablespoon (50 mL) chopped fresh parsley
1 tablespoon (15 mL) chopped fresh thyme
Generous sprinkling of salt
Freshly ground black pepper to taste

Directions

In a large bowl mix together all the ingredients well. Make a tiny patty, fry it up and taste it. You may need to adjust the seasoning. Using wet hands, form 12 even balls of burger mix. Form the balls into patties and arrange on a tray. Separate the layers with wax paper.

I recommend grilling the hamburgers over charcoal, but any other technique will work reasonably well.

Prime Rib of Beef with Two Sauces

Makes 6 servings

The perfect Sunday night roast dinner with the classic combination of horseradish and beef. Leave the leftover beef in the fridge to chill, then slice it thin for delicious sandwiches.

Ingredients

Beef

1 standing rib of beef (5 pounds/2.2 kg),
      at room temperature
1 tablespoon (15 mL) roughly chopped
      fresh thyme
1 tablespoon (15 mL) coarsely ground
      black pepper
2 cloves garlic, finely chopped
2 tablespoons (30 mL) sunflower oil
Salt
1 cup (250 mL) Ontario Cabernet Franc

Parsley-Horseradish Sauce

1 tablespoon (15 mL) butter
1 tablespoon (15 mL) all-purpose flour
1½ cups (375 mL) hot milk
1 bay leaf
1 small onion, peeled
2 whole cloves
1 cup (15 mL) fresh Italian parsley leaves
½ cup (125 mL) grated fresh horseradish,
      plus extra for garnishing
Salt

Directions

Preheat the oven to 350°F (180°C). Rub the beef all over with the thyme, pepper, garlic and oil. Sprinkle liberally with salt. Place the beef fat side up in a roasting pan. Roast, basting periodically, for 15 minutes per pound (500 g) for rare (or 75 minutes) or 18 minutes per pound for medium-rare (90 minutes), or to desired doneness.

Meanwhile, make the sauce. Make a béchamel sauce by melting the butter in a small saucepan over medium heat. Add the flour and stir with a wooden spoon for 5 minutes. Be careful not to let the butter brown. Add the hot milk slowly, stirring constantly to avoid lumps. Fasten the bay leaf to the onion by tacking through the bay leaf with the cloves, and add the onion to the sauce. Reduce heat and simmer for 60 minutes, stirring from time to time.

Meanwhile, add the parsley leaves to a saucepan of boiling water and boil for 10 minutes. Drain the leaves, then purée in a blender.

Pass the béchamel sauce through a fine-mesh strainer. Stir in the puréed parsley and the grated horseradish. Season with salt. Reserve, keeping warm.

Remove the roast to a cutting board. Discard most of the fat from the roasting pan but keep the juices in the pan. Place the roasting pan over medium heat and deglaze with the wine. Boil until the juices have reduced by three-quarters.

Warm 6 plates. Carve a slice of roast onto each plate. Spoon a pool of the pan juices and a pool of the horseradish sauce onto each plate. Grate fresh horseradish onto each plate. Mashed potatoes and roasted root vegetables make a great accompaniment to this dish.

Black and White Braised Beef

Makes 4 servings

Magical harmonies of taste occur between certain ingredients; oysters and Chablis, carrot and ginger, horseradish and beef, corn and beans are all examples of this mysterious and delicious alchemy. "Black and white" refers to the two distinctly different but still harmonious sauces that are part of this presentation.

Ingredients

4 pounds (2 kg) beef short ribs, cut into 4 pieces

2 medium onions, roughly chopped

2 carrots, scrubbed and roughly chopped

2 celery stalks, roughly chopped

4 cloves garlic, thinly sliced

16 black peppercorns, cracked

3 bay leaves

2 whole cloves

2 cups (500 mL) red wine

¼ cup (60 mL) sunflower oil

2 tablespoons (30 mL) tomato paste

4 cups (1 L) strong beef stock

1 tablespoon (15 mL) chopped fresh parsley

Horseradish Béchamel Sauce

2 tablespoons (30 mL) butter

2 tablespoons (30 mL) all-purpose flour

1 medium onion, peeled

3 whole cloves

3 bay leaves

2 cups (500 mL) hot milk

2 tablespoons (30 mL) grated fresh horseradish

1 teaspoon (5 mL) cider vinegar

Salt

recipe continues . . .

Directions

In a large bowl or lidded container, place the short ribs, onions, carrots, celery, garlic, peppercorns, bay leaves, cloves and wine. Cover and refrigerate for 48 hours.

Preheat the oven to 325°F (160°C). Take the ribs out of the marinade and reserve. Strain the marinade into a small saucepan. Reserve the vegetable mixture.

Pour the oil into a roasting pan and place over high heat. Sear the ribs until evenly brown on all sides. Remove from the pan.

Reduce heat to medium and add the reserved vegetables. Sauté until deeply and evenly coloured. Stir in the tomato paste and continue sautéing, stirring regularly, until the tomato paste is almost completely evaporated and is clinging to the vegetables.

Meanwhile, bring the wine to a simmer. Strain the wine through a fine-mesh strainer into the roasting pan and stir, scraping the bottom of the pan. The kitchen will fill with a beautiful aroma of roasting vegetables and boiling wine.

Add the beef stock and return to the boil, then reduce heat to a simmer. Add the ribs and any juices that have accumulated, cover and transfer to the oven. Braise for about 3 hours or until the ribs slide easily away from the meat.

Remove the ribs and reserve, keeping warm. Strain the braising liquid through a fine-mesh strainer into a clean saucepan. Discard the vegetables. Reduce the braising liquid by three-quarters over low heat. Keep warm.

Meanwhile, prepare the horseradish béchamel sauce. In a small saucepan, melt the butter over medium heat. Stir in the flour until smooth, then add the onion, cloves and bay leaves. Gently cook, stirring often, for 10 minutes, being careful not to let anything brown. Slowly add the hot milk, stirring vigorously with a wooden spoon until the sauce is smooth. Cook slowly for about 30 minutes, stirring regularly. If the sauce is too thick, add a little more milk until texture is thick but still flowing. Stir together the horseradish and vinegar, then stir this mixture into the sauce. Season with salt.

Lay out 4 dinner plates. Place a short rib on each plate. Nap each rib with some of the reduced braising liquid. Now nap again with a smooth coating of horseradish béchamel sauce, just enough to cover the top of each rib. Sprinkle with chopped parsley. Serve with boiled potatoes and a nice green salad.

Tamworth piglets from Perth Pork in Sebringville, Ontario;
this heritage breed is part of Slow Food in Canada's Ark of Taste.

Smoked Bacon

Makes 6 servings

Sometimes, even in the middle of the winter, as I am riding my bike to work, I catch the scent of wood smoke on the breeze. As I draw nearer to Gilead the scent is enriched with the emerging smell of bacon. It means Ken Steele is smoking bacon out behind the restaurant. The smell takes the chill out of the ride and makes my mouth water.

Ingredients

1 pound (500 g) kosher salt

8 ounces (250 g) granulated sugar

7 fluid ounces (200 mL) maple syrup

1 piece (4 pounds/2 kg) fresh skin-on pork belly

Directions

Mix together the salt, sugar and maple syrup. In a nonreactive baking dish or roasting pan, spread the salt mixture all around the pork belly. Add enough water to cover the pork. Place an identical baking dish or baking sheet on top of the belly and add about 1 pound (500 g) of weight. Refrigerate for 3 days.

Rinse the salt mixture off the pork belly and dry with paper towels. Hot-smoke with apple wood at 225°F (110°C) for 4 hours or until the internal temperature reaches 180°F (85°C). Let cool.

Bacon can be refrigerated in plastic wrap for 2 months or frozen for 6 months; vacuum-packed, it can be frozen for 1 year.

Confit Pork Belly on Crisp Apple

Makes 6 servings

Before refrigeration, people in southwest France preserved duck and goose for consumption in the winter by slowly cooking it in its own rendered fat and then storing it, completely submerged in that same fat, in a cool place. When required, you simply retrieved a piece from the fat and used it to enhance a dish—cassoulet, for example. As it happens, this is a wonderful way to cook meat, contributing to an extremely tender consistency and rich flavour. I love how cooking the pork belly in this manner allows it to be fried crackling crisp in the final preparation.

Ingredients

8 ounces (250 g) fresh skin-on pork belly
A sprinkling of coarse salt
2 cloves garlic, thinly sliced
2 sprigs of fresh thyme
2 bay leaves
2 cups (500 mL) rendered pork, chicken or duck fat
1 cup (250 mL) simple syrup
1 apple (any kind)
1 shallot, finely chopped
1 tablespoon (15 mL) cider vinegar
1 teaspoon (5 mL) honey
Pinch of salt and freshly ground black pepper

Directions

Combine the pork belly, coarse salt, garlic, thyme and bay leaves in a large bowl. Make sure the salt is evenly distributed over the pork belly. Cover and marinate overnight in the refrigerator.

Preheat the oven to 250°F (120°C). In a flame-proof casserole dish, warm the fat over medium heat until melted. Add the marinated pork to the fat. Cover and cook in the oven for approximately 3 hours or until the belly is extremely tender.

Meanwhile, bring the simple syrup to a simmer in a medium saucepan. Peel and core the apple, then cut in half crosswise. From the wider ends, cut eight rings about ⅛-inch (3 mm) thick. Add the apple rings to the syrup and gently poach for 5 minutes or until tender. Transfer the rings to a baking sheet lined with a nonstick baking mat and place in the oven with the pork belly. Slowly dry the apple rings until they are crispy but not darkening, about 2 hours. Cool on the baking sheet and store in an airtight jar.

Cool the pork belly in the rendered fat, then refrigerate overnight.

Shortly before serving, mix together the shallot, vinegar and honey; season with salt and pepper. Refrigerate.

Remove the confit pork belly from the fat. Cut 6 rectangles of pork belly about ¼ inch (5 mm) thick. Gently fry them in a dry cast-iron frying pan until golden on each side.

Place the apple rings on a platter. Place a crispy pork piece on each ring. Top with some of the shallot mixture and serve.

Refried Beans with Crispy Confit of Pork and Chicken Poached Egg

Makes 6 servings

In 2008, Michael Stadtländer and his wife, Nobuyo, hosted the first Canadian Chefs' Congress at their Eigensinn Farm. Michael had been talking about the importance of connecting chefs from across Canada in a way that would allow them to exchange ideas and to explore opportunities to unite as a single voice on issues that are important to us all. Of course, another great reason to bring like-minded people together is to have fun, and that is one thing cooks know how to do. Especially if there is wine and live music. Chefs came from all over Canada and there was a great lineup of speakers.

Part of the program for that first congress was a "midnight buffet." Several chefs set up cooking stations around a natural amphitheatre on the property. There were wood fires all along the ridge. I set up a large griddle over fire and put together crispy confit of pork and refried bean tacos for everybody.

Poaching eggs in rendered fat is just like poaching in water except the results are much richer.

Ingredients
1 cup (250 mL) dried navy beans, soaked overnight
1¼ cups (300 mL) rendered chicken or duck fat
1 onion, finely chopped
1 leek, diced

6 slices (2 ounces/60 g each) confit pork belly
   (see recipe page 198)
6 eggs
2 tablespoons (30 mL) roughly chopped
   fresh coriander
Salt and freshly ground black pepper

Directions
Drain the beans and simmer in plenty of unsalted water until tender. Drain again.

Place a large frying pan over medium heat. Melt ¼ cup (60 mL) of the rendered fat and gently fry the onion and leek for 5 minutes. Add the drained beans. Continue to fry until the beans start to get a little crunchy on the outside. Transfer to a bowl and keep warm.

In the same pan, gently fry the pork belly until crispy.

Meanwhile, melt the remaining 1 cup (250 mL) rendered fat in a large saucepan over medium heat. Break the eggs one by one into the heated fat. When the whites are cooked but the yolks are still soft, remove the eggs to paper towels to drain.

Set out 6 plates. Stir the coriander into the refried beans and season with salt and pepper. Place some refried beans on each plate. Place a piece of pork belly and a "chicken poached egg" on each plate. Serve.

Individual Tourtière with Mustard Pickle

Makes 6 pies

Sometimes there is nothing I want more than a meat pie. The sandy texture of the sablée pastry and the rich, warmly spiced meat and potato mixture within is so satisfying. I put it on the lunch menu at Gilead, where I serve it with my Aunt Myrtle's mustard pickle. People clamour for these pies. There is a fair amount of preparation to do, but the execution is simple. I make a large batch of pies and freeze them, with excellent results. Sometimes I even serve them in what Ivy insists is the traditional Acadian style, with ketchup.

Ingredients

Pastry
6 cups (750 g) all-purpose flour
1 pound (500 g) lard
Pinch of salt
1 cup (250 mL) cold water
1 egg, lightly beaten, for egg wash

Filling
¼ cup (60 mL) lard
1¼ pounds (625 g) ground pork
2 medium onions, finely chopped
2 medium potatoes, peeled and diced
5 whole allspice, ground
2 whole cloves, ground
Salt and freshly ground black pepper
Aunt Myrtle's Mustard Pickle (see recipe page 294)
    for serving

Directions

To make the pastry, in a large bowl, combine the flour and lard. Using both hands or a pastry blender, cut in the lard until the mixture resembles coarse meal. Dissolve the salt in the cold water and add the water all at once to the flour mixture. Mix the dough just until it comes together. Do not over-mix. Form into a thick log, wrap in plastic and refrigerate for at least 12 hours.

recipe continues . . .

Cut the dough into 12 equal pieces and shape each piece into a ball; wrap and refrigerate 6 of the balls. On a floured surface, roll out the remaining 6 balls into 9-inch (23 cm) circles. Fit each round into a 6-inch (15 cm) pie plate. The dough should hang over the rim slightly. Cover with plastic wrap and refrigerate overnight.

To make the filling, melt the lard in a large frying pan over medium heat. Add the ground pork and gently sauté for about 5 minutes. Add the onions, potatoes, allspice and cloves; continue gently sautéing, stirring regularly, for 20 minutes or until most of the water has evaporated. Season with salt and pepper. Transfer to a bowl, let cool to room temperature, then refrigerate overnight.

Arrange racks in the upper and lower thirds of the oven and preheat the oven to 350°F (180°C).

Set out the 6 pie shells on 2 baking sheets. Divide the meat filling among the shells, mounding it slightly in the centre. Roll out the remaining 6 balls of dough into rounds that will cover the individual pies. Paint a bit of water onto the rim of each pie and place a lid on top. Pinch the lid and the rim of each pie together to seal. Poke a few holes in a decorative fashion on each lid to allow steam to escape. Brush a little egg wash over each pie.

Bake for about 30 minutes or until the pastry is golden brown and the kitchen smells heavenly (or freeze, unbaked, in resealable plastic bags and bake from frozen for about 1 hour). Serve warm or at room temperature with mustard pickle.

Local Food Movement
Dinner—Cumbrae's

Pea and Crab Arancini

Makes 12 arancini

A few years back I was in Italy for Terra Madre, a conference open to Slow Food delegates from all over the world. It coincided with the Salone del Gusto, a wonderful food-and-wine fair that is held every two years in Turin. It is an intense conference, with delegates billeted to wineries and agriturismi in the surrounding Piedmont area. As much networking and trading of stories happened on the bus going to and from the conference as at the conference itself. One day I decided to play hooky and walk around the city. Around five in the afternoon I came upon a square. At one end there was a restaurant that had a wonderful sunny bar area. The staff were putting out platters of snacks on the bar. I asked if there was a private party happening. The waitress said no, this is what they do every day at this time. It is aperitivo! Regulars and new visitors alike come have a drink and a snack and meet their friends. Like a pub, I suppose, but Italian style.

This recipe is an adaptation of a classic Italian aperitivo offering, the arancini, the "little orange." Serve risotto one night to your family or guests, and save the leftovers to turn into these tasty hors d'oeuvres.

Ingredients

1 live large Dungeness crab (or 5 ounces/150 g thawed frozen crab meat)

1 cup (250 mL) leftover risotto

1 tablespoon (15 mL) chopped fresh parsley

1 tablespoon (15 mL) cider mayonnaise (see recipe page 348)

1 egg, beaten

1 cup (250 mL) dry breadcrumbs or panko

2 cups (500 mL) sunflower oil

Directions

If you are using a live crab, plunge the crab into boiling salted water and cook, covered, for about 8 minutes. Remove with tongs and let cool. When cool enough to handle, crack shells and remove all the meat. (A tedious task.)

Mix crab meat with the risotto, parsley and mayonnaise. Form the rice mixture into 12 balls the size of a large gumball. Dip each ball into the beaten egg, then roll in the breadcrumbs to coat. If not cooking immediately, reserve in the refrigerator for up to 12 hours.

When you are ready to serve, heat the oil in a large saucepan to about 325°F (160°C). Fry the arancini, a few at a time, until golden brown, about 3 minutes. Drain on paper towels and serve while still warm.

Smoked Whitefish Canapé

Makes 12 canapés

As an apprentice cook, on my way to work each morning I would pass by the Danish Food Centre at the corner of Bloor and St. Thomas Streets. It was a busy lunch restaurant, serving up myriad open-faced sandwiches. There were shrimp, herring, mackerel and egg salad preparations, all beautifully displayed in a glass-fronted vitrine. This canapé takes it inspiration from that memory. In my search for sourcing local ingredients first for recipes, smoked whitefish was an obvious choice.

Ingredients

½ medium fennel bulb, thinly sliced

¼ medium white onion, thinly sliced

¼ medium red onion, thinly sliced

2 green onions, thinly sliced

2 tablespoons (30 mL) white wine vinegar

1 tablespoon (15 mL) chopped fresh dill

Salt and freshly ground black pepper

2 tablespoons (30 mL) butter, softened

3 slices (¼ inch/5 mm thick) artisanal sourdough
   bread

1 pound (500 g) smoked whitefish (or any other
   smoked fish), skin removed and thinly sliced

2 tablespoons (30 mL) crème fraîche or sour cream

12 small sprigs of fresh dill or thin green onion
   slices, for garnishing

Directions

In a large bowl, combine the fennel, white onion, red onion, green onions, white wine vinegar and chopped dill. Mix together and add salt and pepper to taste.

Spread butter on one side of each slice of bread. Spread the fennel and onion salad on top of the bread slices. Cover the salad with slices of smoked whitefish. Using a knife, trim the edges so that each slice has the fish and salad right to the edge. Cut each slice into 4 squares. Dollop a small amount of crème fraîche on each canapé and garnish as desired.

Consommé of Beef with Marrow Quenelles

Makes 6 servings

I remember James Chatto reviewing my restaurant Palmerston. He must have tasted my consommé then, because later when he wrote *The Man Who Ate Toronto*, he said that in the '80s, I was known as Mr. Consommé. There is something about the intense flavour and distillation process of making a consommé that has always intrigued me. I remember my mother administering Campbell's consommé to me as a child when I was sick. This version is much, much better. You can serve this flavourful soup without the quenelles and it will still be memorably satisfying.

Ingredients
Consommé

2 onions, peeled and halved crosswise

1 pound (500 g) ground shank of beef

1 carrot, diced

1 leek, diced

1 small celery stalk, peeled and diced

2 cloves garlic, diced

3 bay leaves

2 whole cloves

½ whole nutmeg, grated

20 black peppercorns, coarsely ground

1 sprig of fresh thyme

4 egg whites

2 tablespoons (30 mL) tomato paste

Salt

8 cups (2 L) strong beef stock

Quenelles

3½ ounces (100 g) beef shank meat

1 ice cube

2 ounces (60 g) beef bone marrow

1 egg yolk

3 tablespoons (50 g) butter, softened

1 tablespoon (15 mL) cognac

2 tablespoons (30 mL) chopped fresh parsley

1 tablespoon (15 mL) chopped fresh thyme

½ teaspoon (2 mL) freshly grated nutmeg

3 tablespoons (50 mL) whipping cream

Salt

Garnish

3½ ounces (100 g) thinly sliced mushrooms

12 slices beef bone marrow

4 green onions, thinly sliced

3½ ounces (100 g) raw beef tenderloin,
    thinly sliced

Directions
To make the consommé, cook the onion halves cut side down over a gas flame or in a dry frying pan over high heat until burnt. Dice the onions and put them in a large bowl. Add the beef, carrot, leek, celery, garlic, bay leaves, cloves, nutmeg, peppercorns, thyme, egg whites, tomato paste and salt to taste. Mix together well.

Transfer the mixture to a large soup pot and add the beef stock. Mix well. Slowly bring to the boil, stirring regularly. Once the egg white "raft" is set on top, reduce to a simmer and allow the liquid to percolate for approximately 1 hour.

Using a ladle, carefully strain the consommé through a fine-mesh strainer into a clean pot. Do not press on the solids. Bring just to a simmer before serving.

To make the quenelles, process the shank meat with the ice cube in a food processor. Add the marrow, egg yolk, butter, cognac, parsley, thyme and nutmeg; process until smooth, about 30 seconds. While the processor is running, slowly add the cream. Season with salt to taste.

Heat 6 soup bowls. Fill a medium saucepan with water and bring to the boil. Drop 12 teaspoon-sized quenelles into the boiling water and cook until they float to the surface, about 1 minute. Remove to a plate using a slotted spoon.

Place 2 quenelles in each soup bowl. Divide the sliced mushrooms, bone marrow, green onions and tenderloin slices equally among the bowls. Pour hot consommé into each bowl and serve immediately.

215

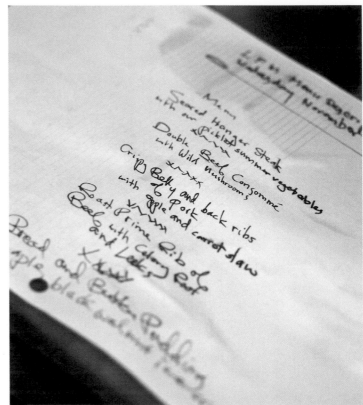

Bread and Butter Pudding with Maple Walnut Ice Cream

Makes 8 servings

This is a homespun classic and a good way to make use of stale bread and cake. Keep a container going in the freezer until you collect about 2 cups (500 mL) of crustless cake or bread cut into small cubes. We like to serve our house-made maple walnut ice cream with this pudding, but a pint from your local ice-cream maker will pair nicely as well.

Ingredients

7 eggs

⅔ cup (150 g) + 1 tablespoon (15 mL) granulated
  sugar

2½ cups (625 mL) whole milk

1⅔ cups (400 mL) whipping cream

1 teaspoon (5 mL) vanilla extract

Pinch of salt

1 tablespoon (15 mL) butter

2 cups (500 mL) cubed bread or cake

3 tablespoons (50 mL) raisins, rehydrated in water
  and drained

6 tablespoons (90 mL) apricot jam, melted

Directions

In a large bowl, whisk together the eggs and ⅔ cup (150 g) sugar. Add the milk, cream, vanilla and salt and mix well.

Grease a 9-inch (2.5 L) square baking dish with the butter and sprinkle bottom and sides with 1 tablespoon (15 mL) granulated sugar. Place the cubed bread and soaked raisins in the dish. Pour the egg mixture on top and let sit until the egg mixture is well absorbed.

Meanwhile, preheat the oven to 325°F (160°C). Bake the pudding for about 1 hour or until a cake tester comes out clean. Spread the melted jam over the surface and bake for an additional 15 minutes to form a glaze. Let cool for 30 minutes before serving.

Portion onto 8 plates. Serve with a dollop of maple walnut ice cream on the side.

Fish

These photographs were taken at Purdy Fisheries in Port Thomas, Ontario, when Jamie,
Ivy and I took a day trip together for a tour and visit with Steph Purdy.
After spending the last few years working for Jamie, I've come to the conclusion that his work with
lake fish is one of his most significant contributions to local cuisine.

JO DICKINS, ASSISTANT, PHOTOGRAPHER

Chefs like Jamie give validation to how we handle our fish and to how we do business.
They bring their expertise to the lesser-known species like channel cats, freshwater drum
and silver bass, and they elevate something that one person may see as "junk" and
make it something beautiful. We all know that at one time bologna cost more than lobster,
and Patagonian toothfish, a.k.a. Chilean sea bass, was once considered a junk fish.

STEPH PURDY, PURDY FISHERIES

Marinated Herring with Warm Apple and Potato Salad

Makes 4 servings

When I cater large events, or any event for that matter, I always try to make sure that the dishes I provide capture something of the spirit of the event or the client I am working with. In this case the clients came from northern Germany, and so I wanted to express something of my impression of the North Sea and the culture of that area.

Ingredients

Marinated Herring
4 fresh herring fillets
Coarse sea salt
1 cup (250 mL) sweet apple cider
3 tablespoons (50 mL) cider vinegar
3 tablespoons (50 mL) finely diced shallots
Coarsely ground black pepper

Salad
5 medium Yukon Gold potatoes
1 Golden Delicious apple, peeled, cored and sliced
1 onion, thinly sliced
2 dill pickles, cut into julienne
2 tablespoons (30 mL) pickle juice
2 tablespoons (30 mL) Dijon mustard
2 tablespoons (30 mL) sunflower oil
3 tablespoons (50 mL) chopped fresh parsley
1 tablespoon (15 mL) chopped fresh thyme
Salt and freshly ground black pepper

Directions

To marinate the herring, lay the herring fillets flesh side up on a plate. Sprinkle liberally with coarse sea salt. Cover and refrigerate for 6 hours.

Rinse the fillets under cold water and dry them on paper towels.

Simmer the apple cider until syrupy and reduced to 3 tablespoons (50 mL). Be careful not to caramelize it, as this will remove the delicate apple flavour. Remove from the heat and stir in the cider vinegar and the diced shallots.

Lay the dried fillets flesh side up in a ceramic or glass dish. Spoon the shallot mixture evenly over the fillets. Sprinkle the black pepper on top. Leave at room temperature while you prepare the salad.

Place the potatoes in a saucepan and cover with cold water. Add salt. Bring to the boil and cook until tender, about 30 minutes.

Meanwhile, in a medium bowl, combine the apple, onion, pickles, pickle juice, mustard, sunflower oil, parsley and thyme. Toss well.

Drain the potatoes and leave to cool for 10 minutes. Peel them and slice into rounds. Add to the apple mixture, mix well and season with salt and pepper.

Spoon some salad onto 4 plates. Drape a marinated herring fillet over each mound of salad. Spoon some shallot mixture on top of the salad. Serve.

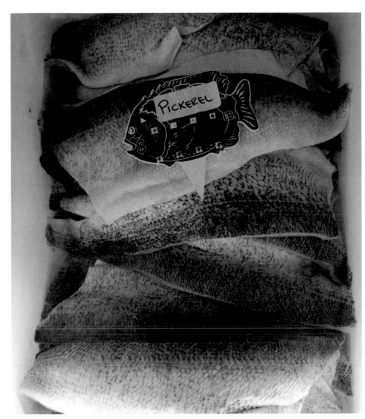

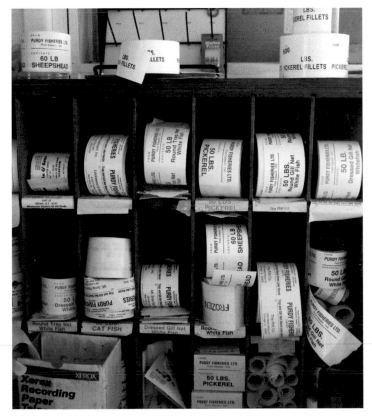

Blini with Smoked Whitefish and Whitefish Roe

Makes 12 servings

I met Andrew and Natasha Akiwenzie at the Riverdale Farmers' Market through Elizabeth Harris, the woman largely responsible for the resurgence of farmers' markets in Toronto. They and their family live on Cape Croker up on the Bruce Peninsula, near Georgian Bay. Andrew fishes for whitefish primarily, although I have seen him bring chinook salmon to the market from time to time. I am so fortunate to be able to offer this fish to my customers and to see their delight when eating it. In addition to helping Andrew prepare the fish for market, Natasha also prepares the roe. As with the fish itself, I had never experienced whitefish roe tasting this delicious and being so finely textured. Good thing, because it is a painstaking task to prepare it.

Whitefish roe from the Akiwenzies may not be readily available, so try this recipe with whitefish roe from another source or even substitute salmon eggs. Or, if you are really feeling flush, there are a couple of enterprises that have started up in the last decade on both the east and west coasts that prepare caviar from sturgeon, the original. New Brunswick's Acadian Sturgeon is a favourite.

Ingredients

1 cup (250 mL) milk, warmed to 120°F (50°C)
¼ cup (60 mL) butter, softened
2 eggs, lightly beaten
1 teaspoon (5 mL) active dry yeast
Pinch of nutmeg
Pinch of salt
½ cup (50 g) sifted unbleached pastry flour
1 tablespoon (15 mL) buckwheat flour
½ cup (125 mL) fennel and onion salad
   (see recipe page 212)
½ pound (250 g) smoked whitefish, sliced
½ cup (125 mL) crème fraîche or sour cream
4 ounces (125 g) whitefish roe
¼ cup (60 mL) finely chopped chives

Directions

Combine the warm milk and butter in a medium bowl and stir until the butter is melted. Whisk in the eggs, yeast, nutmeg and salt. Sift in the pastry flour and the buckwheat flour, stirring just enough to combine. Do not over-mix. As the yeast develops, the blini batter will come together on its own. Cover with plastic wrap and leave at room temperature to develop for 2 hours.

Heat a dry nonstick frying pan over medium heat. Do not stir the batter at this stage because you want to preserve the natural leavening effect of the yeast to create light, airy blinis. Gently drop the batter by the tablespoonful into the pan to make silver-dollar-size pancakes and cook until golden brown. Lay the blinis out on a serving dish.

Place a spoonful of the fennel and onion salad on each blini. Top with smoked whitefish, a small dollop of crème fraîche and a good amout of whitefish roe. Garnish the plate with chives, and serve.

223

Escabeche of Whitefish

Makes 6 servings

In the restaurant world, a concept for a new dish must be considered in the context of how well that dish can be executed during a busy dinner service. I remember a good example of this when I had the Wine Bar. We were running an artisanal cheese plate on the menu, served with wild rice roti as a vehicle for the cheese. The roti, while delicious and a wonderful complement to the cheeses, simply did not work well in the service context. It took too long to bake them to order. Many unhappy customers later, the roti evolved to a different form. We began serving wild rice crackers with the cheeses instead. This was a boon for service, as the crackers could be prepared ahead of time and the cracker itself drew raves from our customers for its earthy taste and soft, crunchy texture. I continue to serve wild rice crackers with our cheeses to this day (see recipe page 263). Escabeche is also a technique that can be done ahead of time so that come serving time, it is just a matter of assembling a few elements and the dish is ready to go.

Ingredients

¼ cup (60 mL) white wine vinegar

1 tablespoon (15 mL) honey

Juice of 2 lemons

1 red onion, thinly sliced

1 small green chili, finely chopped, seeds and all

1 tablespoon (15 mL) roughly chopped fresh coriander

Salt and freshly ground black pepper

¼ cup (60 mL) sunflower oil

12 slices (2 ounces/60 g each) fresh skin-on pickerel or whitefish fillet

1 small bunch of fresh coriander

Directions

In a medium bowl, stir together the vinegar, honey and lemon juice. Add the red onion, chili, chopped coriander, and salt and pepper to taste. Transfer this marinade to an oblong baking dish.

Add the sunflower oil to a large frying pan and place it over medium heat. Season the slices of fish on both sides with salt. Fry the fish slowly until golden brown on both sides. Transfer the fillets as they are cooked to the baking dish and nestle them in the marinade. Let the fish marinate for 1 hour. Serve at room temperature with a nice potato salad, or, as shown here, with steamed root vegetables and niçoise olives.

Sunflower-Poached Whitefish with Hillier Soubise

Makes 6 servings

Fully engaging in local food procurement practices is a process that takes many years. As time passes, one becomes better connected to sources of supply. I first started using sunflower oil in the kitchen twenty years ago, when I discovered that peanut oil caused allergic reactions in an increasing number of my customers. Since then, I've found a great source for sunflower oil from Cobourg, Ontario. My cousin and his son are growing and pressing their own. "Hillier" is a reference to the onions from my farm in Prince Edward County. It's one of the farm's most successful crops.

Ingredients

¾ cup (190 g) butter
4 medium onions, thinly sliced
1 tablespoon (15 mL) cider vinegar
Salt
4 cups (1 L) sunflower oil
4 fresh whitefish fillets (5 ounces/150 g each)
2 tablespoons (30 mL) olive oil
2 shallots
1 bunch of spinach
Freshly ground black pepper

Directions

Melt the butter in a large saucepan over medium-low heat. Add the onions and sauté slowly for approximately 30 minutes. Transfer the onions to a blender and process on high speed until smooth. Add the vinegar and season with salt. Reserve the soubise.

Warm 4 dinner plates.

Heat the sunflower oil in a medium saucepan to approximately 160°F (70°C). Add the fillets of fish. Remove from the heat and allow fillets to poach in the warm oil until opaque and flaky, about 10 minutes. Remove fillets with a slotted spoon and drain on paper towels.

In a large frying pan, heat the olive oil over medium-high heat. Add the shallots and sauté until golden brown. Add the spinach and sauté for 3 minutes. Season with salt and pepper.

Spoon soubise into the centre of each plate. Place some sautéed spinach on top of each pool of soubise. Place the cooked fish on the spinach. Serve immediately.

Fried Fish Cakes with Chili Mayonnaise

Makes 6 servings

A few years ago, I was cooking at a premiers' conference in Niagara-on-the-Lake. It was a beautiful summer evening. The event was held outdoors with all the premiers of our provinces and territories wandering about, enjoying themselves. There were salads and grilled fish and then, of course, a beautiful Niagara peach dessert. At the end of the evening I was presented with a lovely souvenir of the day. It was a picnic suitcase that opened up to reveal a place setting for four complete with wine glasses, a corkscrew and a cheese board and knife. I think of these fish cakes as the perfect picnic food, and I made them the first time I used my picnic suitcase.

Ingredients

Poached Fish

1 carrot, thinly sliced

1 onion, thinly sliced

1 celery stalk, thinly sliced

2 tablespoons (30 mL) white wine vinegar

2 bay leaves

6 black peppercorns

Salt

4 cups (1 L) water

1 pound (500 g) fresh skinless whitefish or
   pickerel fillets

Fish Cakes

1 large Yukon Gold potato

2 shallots, finely chopped

Juice of 1 lemon

1 egg, lightly beaten

2 tablespoons (30 mL) cider mayonnaise
   (see recipe page 348)

1 tablespoon (15 mL) white wine vinegar

2 tablespoons (30 mL) finely chopped fresh chives

2 tablespoons (30 mL) chopped fresh parsley

1 teaspoon (5 mL) roughly chopped fresh tarragon

Salt and freshly ground black pepper

4 cups (1 L) sunflower oil

1 cup (250 mL) all-purpose flour

1 egg, beaten

2 cups (500 mL) panko or dry breadcrumbs

12 lemon wedges

¾ cup (175 mL) chili mayonnaise
   (see recipe page 349)

Directions

To poach the fish, in a large pot, combine the carrot, onion, celery, vinegar, bay leaves, peppercorns, salt to taste and the water. Boil for 5 minutes over high heat, then reduce heat to a simmer and add the fish. Simmer for 10 minutes or until fish is opaque throughout. Remove pot from heat and allow fish to cool to room temperature in the court bouillon.

recipe continues . . .

229

Meanwhile, to make the fish cakes, in a separate pot, boil the potato until tender. Peel, then rice the potato into a medium bowl. Add the shallots, lemon juice, egg, mayonnaise, vinegar, chives, parsley, tarragon, and salt and pepper to taste.

Remove the fish from the court bouillon and pat it dry with paper towels. Discard bouillon. Using your hands, flake the fish into the potato mixture. Mix well. Shape the mixture into 12 patties. Refrigerate for 2 hours.

In a large saucepan over medium heat, heat the sunflower oil to 350°F (180°C).

Dip the fish cakes, one at a time, first in the flour, then in the beaten egg and finally in the panko, coating well. Lay the breaded fish cakes on a baking sheet until the oil has reached frying temperature.

Fry the fish cakes, two or three at a time, turning frequently, until golden brown on both sides. Drain on paper towels. When they have cooled to room temperature they may be packed in an airtight container to take on your picnic. Pack the lemon wedges and chili mayonnaise separately.

Courtship Pickerel

Makes 2 servings

When I was seventeen and thinking about getting into cooking as a profession, I kept coming across words like *apprenticeship* and *journeyman*. I fantasized about travelling the world with my knife kit tucked under my arm. This fantasy more or less came true in the years following my apprenticeship in Toronto, when I indeed did become a journeyman and did travel the world. I met many people and learned many things. I remember in Paris hanging out with my Moroccan friends and learning of the rich and robust flavours of Moroccan cuisine.

Fast-forward thirty years and I find myself searching my memory for a dish with flavours so seductive and surprising that the woman of my dreams simply could not resist its charms and my advances. I land on the memory of a fish dish that many of us shared sitting on the floor and eating with our hands from large round pounded-brass trays. The usual animated conversation now hushed, our attention riveted on savouring these irresistible flavours. The courtship continues.

Ingredients

4 pieces (1½ ounces/50 g each) fresh pickerel
Salt
Juice of 1 lemon
1 tablespoon (15 mL) roughly chopped fresh
    coriander
1 clove garlic, finely minced

2 tablespoons (30 mL) white wine vinegar
1 tablespoon (15 mL) cumin seeds, lightly toasted
    and ground
1 tablespoon (15 mL) sweet paprika
1 teaspoon (5 mL) Hungarian hot paprika
2 tablespoons (30 mL) all-purpose flour
2 cups (500 mL) sunflower oil
2 lemon wedges for garnishing
2 big sprigs of fresh coriander for garnishing

Directions

Season the fillets of pickerel with salt.

In a shallow bowl, whisk together the lemon juice, chopped coriander, garlic, vinegar, cumin seeds and the sweet and hot paprika. Add the fish to the marinade, turning to coat. Cover and refrigerate overnight.

Remove the fillets from the marinade. Whisk the flour into the marinade to make a thin paste.

Place the oil in a large pot and heat over medium heat to 350°F (180°C).

Working with two pieces at a time, dip the fillets in the marinade paste, evenly coating them, and place them carefully in the hot oil. Cook for about 5 minutes, flipping them once halfway through, until crispy. Drain on paper towels.

Arrange fillets on 2 plates. Garnish each with a wedge of lemon and a generous sprig of fresh coriander. Serve.

Steamed Filled Whole Pickerel with Dill Sauce

Makes 10 servings

This is a great dish for a large group of people. It is also probably the most difficult recipe to prepare in this book. I include it here because I think many readers—professional chefs and advanced home cooks—might enjoy the challenge of preparing it.

I was inspired to create this dish by a talented chef and garde manger I knew at the beginning of my career. His name is Fred Reindl and he had come to Canada from Germany. He prepared a filled-pike dish for a culinary competition in Chicago. I was there assisting my chef, Ulrich Herzig, at the same competition. I was struck by the beauty of the finished dish and the complexity of its preparation. Although pike is traditionally the fish used in this dish, I prefer to use pickerel, as it is more readily available and so far is still a sustainable option in our Great Lakes fishery.

Ingredients

Steamed Whole Pickerel

1 whole fresh pickerel (about 3 pounds/1.5 kg), scaled and gutted

4 ice cubes

5 tablespoons (90 g) butter, softened

4 egg yolks

1 clove garlic, finely minced

1 tablespoon (15 mL) pastis or other anise liqueur

6 tablespoons (90 mL) whipping cream

Salt

1 carrot, diced, blanched for 5 minutes and cooled

2 tablespoons (30 mL) chopped fresh dill

Dill Sauce

1 cup (250 mL) whipping cream

1 fennel bulb, thinly sliced

1 onion, thinly sliced

1 celery stalk, thinly sliced

1 bay leaf

2 tablespoons (30 mL) finely chopped fresh dill

1 cup (250 mL) white wine

Mignonette

2 shallots, finely chopped

1 teaspoon (5 mL) finely chopped chives

1 teaspoon (5 mL) finely chopped parsley

3 tablespoons (45 mL) white wine vinegar

Freshly ground black pepper

recipe continues . . .

233

Directions

Using a filleting knife, very carefully remove the skeletal structure from the fish, leaving the fish whole and the skin unbroken. This is a tedious but not impossible task and is the key to this dish's success. You can also ask your fishmonger to do this for you. Reserve the bones.

Carefully pare away approximately half of the flesh from each fillet. Cut this flesh into small pieces and place in the freezer for about 30 minutes to firm up. Meanwhile, keep the boned-out fish in the refrigerator.

Place half of the firmed-up pickerel flesh in a food processor. Add 2 of the ice cubes. Process until smooth. While the processor is running, start adding half of the butter bit by bit. While continuing to run the processor, add 2 of the egg yolks, half of the garlic and half of the pastis. With the processor still running, add 3 tablespoons (50 mL) of the cream in a steady stream. Add salt to taste. Transfer this fish mousse to a bowl. Process the other half of the mousse ingredients in the same manner and add to the bowl. Stir the carrot and chopped dill into the mousse. Season with salt. Refrigerate for 30 minutes.

Spread the fish out flesh side up on a sheet of plastic wrap. Spread the fish mousse lengthwise along the centre of the fish. Draw up the plastic wrap to close the fillets around the filling. Tie the ends of the plastic wrap, forming a tight cylinder. Refrigerate for 2 hours.

To make the dill sauce, gently boil the cream in a small saucepan until reduced by half.

Cut up the reserved fish bones and place them in a medium saucepan. Add the fennel, onion, celery, bay leaf, dill and white wine. Bring to the boil, then reduce heat to a simmer. Stir in the reduced cream and simmer for an additional 5 minutes. Discard bay leaf. Transfer to a food processor and process until smooth.

Force this mixture through a fine-mesh strainer back into the saucepan, pressing on the solids to extract as much liquid as possible. Discard the solids.

Meanwhile, add enough water to cover the bottom of a fish poacher. Place the plastic-wrapped pickerel on the perforated insert and lower it into the pan. Place the poacher over medium heat and bring to the boil. Cover the pot and steam the pickerel for approximately 20 minutes or until a thermometer inserted into the centre of the filling reads 140°F (60°C). Lift the fish and the insert onto the counter. Unwrap the fish.

Meanwhile, bring the sauce to a simmer.

To make the mignonette, in a small bowl place the shallots, chives, parsley, white wine vinegar and pepper to taste. Stir to combine.

Lay out 10 plates. Spoon some dill sauce onto each plate. Using a sharp serrated knife, carefully cut 10 slices of the filled pickerel. Place a slice on each plate. Garnish with a spoonful of mignonette and serve.

Refrigerate leftovers and consume within a day.

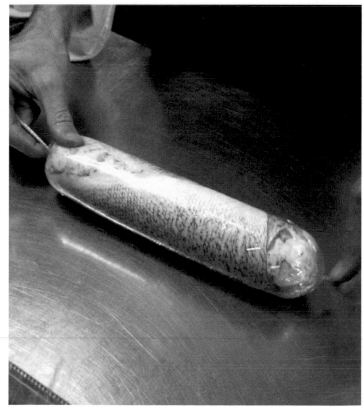

Wild Rice Perch Meunière "Salad" with Lemon and Wild Watercress

Makes 6 servings

When the transformation of the ROM began, my restaurant had a date with the wrecking ball. One of the things I salvaged was a beautiful griddle made of 1-inch steel plate. I made a structure out of field-stone at Michael Stadtländer's Eigensinn Farm that housed a rudimentary firebox that in turn heated the griddle that fried the fish for this recipe.

Ingredients

Lemon Beurre Blanc

2 cups (500 mL) dry white wine

7 tablespoons (100 mL) white wine vinegar

3 shallots, thinly sliced

1 bay leaf

12 black peppercorns, crushed

¾ cup (190 g) cold butter, cut into small cubes

⅓ cup (75 mL) fresh lemon juice

Fish

12 fresh skinless yellow perch fillets

Salt and freshly ground black pepper

⅔ cup (100 g) wild rice flour

½ cup (125 mL) clarified butter

Salad

2 bunches watercress (preferably wild-harvested, though cultivated will do in a pinch), washed and dried

1 jar (1 pint/500 mL) pickled wild mushrooms (see recipe page 289), drained

Directions

To make the lemon beurre blanc, place the white wine, white wine vinegar, shallots, bay leaf and peppercorns in a small nonreactive saucepan. Bring to the boil, then reduce heat and gently simmer until the liquid is syrupy. Remove from the heat and whisk in the cold butter all at once until completely melted and the sauce is emulsified, returning the pot to the element briefly to help melt the butter. Discard the bay leaf. Transfer the sauce to a blender. While the blender is running at high speed, gradually add the lemon juice. Strain through a fine-mesh strainer and reserve in a warm place.

Pat the fish fillets dry with a paper towel. Season with salt and pepper. Pour the wild rice flour into a pie plate and dredge the fish on both sides.

In a large cast-iron frying pan, heat the clarified butter over medium-high heat until it begins to smoke. Add the perch fillets and sauté for 1 minute on each side. Transfer to a plate lined with paper towels.

Arrange the watercress and pickled mushrooms on 6 salad plates. Arrange 2 fillets per person in among the salad. Nap each fillet with a small amount of lemon beurre blanc.

238

Beer-Battered Georgian Bay Perch with Wild Leek Tartar Sauce

Makes 6 servings

This recipe will work with any locally caught lake fish. I like to support the incredible craft brewers we have in this province. The beer adds a great flavour dimension as well as contributing to the light texture of the batter.

Ingredients

Tartar Sauce

1¼ cups (300 mL) cider mayonnaise (see recipe page 348) or store-bought
¼ bunch of fresh Italian parsley
5 wild leek bulbs (or 3 green onions), finely chopped
2 tablespoons (30 mL) chopped capers
2 tablespoons (30 mL) chopped dill pickle
Lemon juice
Salt

Fish

3 eggs
1 bottle of your favourite local craft beer
¼ teaspoon (1 mL) freshly grated nutmeg
Salt
3¼ cups (300 g) pastry flour, sifted
12 cups (3 L) sunflower oil
18 fresh skinless yellow perch fillets
All-purpose flour for dredging

Directions

To make the tartar sauce, in a bowl, stir together the mayonnaise, parsley, wild leeks, capers and pickles until well combined. Season with lemon juice and salt. Refrigerate until needed.

For the fish, separate the eggs into 2 medium bowls. Whip the egg whites with a whisk until they form soft peaks. To the egg yolks, add the beer, nutmeg and salt to taste. Add the flour gradually, mixing gently with the whisk. Fold in the egg whites and place the batter in the refrigerator until the oil is hot.

Heat the oil in a large pot to 350°F (180°C).

Dredge the fish in the flour and then dip through the batter, making sure each fillet is completely coated. Feather the coated fillet through the hot oil (drag the fillet lightly through the oil) before releasing into the pot. Fry in batches of 6 until the fillets are golden brown. Drain on paper towels.

Serve with the tartar sauce, your favourite cole slaw and french fries or potato salad.

239

Pan-Fried Yellow Perch with Fresh Sorrel and New Potatoes

Makes 4 servings

I like to serve sorrel with fish. It is a puckery, lemony, refreshing green. It really adds a distinctive zing to the finished dish.

Ingredients

Sorrel Purée

2 onions, finely chopped
⅔ cup (150 g) butter
1 medium potato (any kind), peeled and
    cut into large dice
2 handfuls fresh sorrel leaves
⅔ cup (150 mL) chicken stock
Freshly grated nutmeg
Salt and freshly ground black pepper

Potatoes

8 small new potatoes
Salt

Fish

¼ cup (60 mL) butter
8 fresh skin-on yellow perch fillets (pickerel
    or whitefish will also do marvellously)
All-purpose flour for dredging
Salt and freshly ground black pepper

Directions

To make the sorrel purée, gently sauté the onions in the butter in a medium saucepan for 10 minutes. Add the potatoes and continue to sauté for 3 more minutes. Add the sorrel leaves and the chicken stock. Bring to the boil, stirring from time to time. Reduce heat to a simmer and season with the nutmeg, salt and pepper to taste. Transfer to a food processor and purée. Reserve, keeping warm.

Boil the new potatoes in salted water until they are tender, approximately 15 minutes. Drain, return to the pot and keep warm.

For the fish, melt the butter in a large frying pan over medium heat. When the butter is sizzling, dredge the fillets one by one in the flour and place in the sizzling butter. Cook, turning once, until crispy and golden on both sides.

Meanwhile, warm 4 dinner plates. Divide the sorrel purée among the plates. Place 2 fillets of fried perch in the centre of each plate. Place 2 potatoes on either side of the fish on each plate. Serve immediately.

Pristine Poached Halibut with Spot Prawn Sauce

Makes 4 servings

For two summers in a row I had the good fortune to be invited as guest chef at the West Coast Fishing Club. The club is situated in the wilderness outside Masset in the Haida Gwaii. The first year, I took my son Jackson with me, and the second year, I took my son Nile. Both trips will be remembered forever. The land and the ocean and the spirituality of the place linger. I hope to get back there someday. Guests of the club would sally forth each morning to fish for salmon, mostly chinook, and halibut. I was interested in exploring what else there might be and set about foraging on the beach, delving a bit deeper. Ken Beatty—Captain Ken as he was known—ran the outpost and knew a lot about what other foods could be caught or foraged in that area. He pried rock scallops from the craggy rock in the bay and set traps for spot prawns. This recipe is emblematic of those outpost experiences.

Spot prawn season is short. They are available fresh from late May until late June. They are also available frozen year round from a good fishmonger.

I often serve this fish on a bed of braised greens. Simply place a mound of seasoned braised greens (kale, chard) atop the sauce and place fish atop greens.

Ingredients

¼ cup (60 mL) olive oil
½ teaspoon (2 mL) caraway seeds
1 onion, thinly sliced
1 fennel bulb, thinly sliced
1 leek, thinly sliced
2 cloves garlic, thinly sliced
20 fresh (preferably live) spot prawns
1 tablespoon (15 mL) tomato paste
½ cup (125 mL) white wine
    (reserve 1 tablespoon/15 mL)
2 cups (500 mL) fish or chicken stock
Salt
About 3 cups (750 mL) cold-pressed non-
    genetically-modified soybean oil
4 fresh skinless halibut fillets (4 ounces/125 g each)
Fleur de sel or flaky sea salt for serving

Directions

Heat the olive oil in a large pot over medium heat. Add the caraway seeds, onion, fennel, leek and garlic. Sweat for 5 minutes without colouring.

Add the spot prawns. Cover and steam for 4 minutes or until they turn bright orange. Remove the pot from the heat. When the prawns are cool enough to handle, separate the tail meat and reserve in the refrigerator.

recipe continues . . .

243

Place the pot back on medium heat and add the prawn shells. Simmer for an additional 5 minutes. Stir in the tomato paste. Increase the heat while stirring regularly with a wooden spoon to deepen the colour of the mixture and to "roast" the tomato paste. This should take about 10 minutes. You want to deepen the colour evenly, not burn anything.

Add the white wine and let the alcohol burn off, about 1 minute. Add the stock, reduce the heat and simmer for 5 minutes.

Transfer the mixture to a food processor and process to a purée. Force the purée through a fine-mesh strainer into a saucepan, using a ladle to press on the solids. Season with salt. Bring the prawn sauce to the boil, then turn off the heat and cover.

Pour enough soybean oil into a large saucepan to completely submerge the halibut fillets. Slowly heat the oil to 140°F (60°C). Place the fillets in the warmed oil and poach them for about 8 minutes or until the flesh is beginning to become opaque.

Meanwhile, heat the prawn tail meat with the reserved 1 tablespoon (15 mL) white wine in a small saucepan, covered. Reheat the prawn sauce at the same time.

Pour 2 tablespoons (30 mL) of prawn sauce onto each of 4 plates. Arrange 5 prawns in a pleasing pattern on each plate. Lift the halibut fillets out of the oil with a slotted spoon and place a fillet on top of the sauce on each plate. Sprinkle each fillet with some fleur de sel. Serve.

Lobster Éclairs

Makes 12 éclairs

I once catered an event where I wanted to serve a cold lobster salad. I was trying to figure out the vehicle for presentation. I didn't want something too bready, and so I landed on éclair pastry, or pâte à choux. It worked out beautifully, carrying the filling well and allowing the richness of the lobster to shine.

When buying lobster, ask the fishmonger to select lively female specimens. They are the most delicious.

Ingredients

Pâte à Choux

2½ cups (200 g) sifted pastry flour
Pinch of freshly grated nutmeg
Pinch of salt
6 tablespoons (100 g) butter
7 fluid ounces (200 mL) milk
3 eggs

Lobster Filling

3 tablespoons (50 mL) salt
3 live lobsters (1¼ pounds/625 g each)
½ cup (125 mL) cider mayonnaise
   (see recipe page 348)
6 tablespoons (90 mL) finely chopped fresh fennel
1 teaspoon (5 mL) chopped fresh parsley
1 teaspoon (5 mL) chopped fresh chives
1 teaspoon (5 mL) chopped fresh chervil
½ teaspoon (2 mL) chopped fresh tarragon
Juice of ½ lemon
Salt and freshly ground black pepper
24 arugula leaves

Directions

Preheat the oven to 300°F (150°C). Line a baking sheet with parchment paper or a nonstick baking mat.

To make the pâte à choux, stir together the flour, nutmeg and salt. Bring the butter and milk to the boil in a small saucepan over medium heat. Add the flour mixture all at once and stir vigorously with a wooden spoon until the mixture comes together in a ball. Remove from the heat. Add the eggs, one at a time, stirring vigorously after each addition until the mixture is well blended and smooth.

246

Using a piping bag fitted with a large plain tip, pipe 12 cigar-shaped strips, each 5 inches (12 cm) long, onto the baking sheet, leaving 2 inches (5 cm) between each éclair. Bake until golden brown and crisp, about 15 to 20 minutes. Allow to cool completely on a rack.

For the lobster filling, bring a large pot of water to the boil over high heat. When the water reaches the boil, add the salt. Place the lobsters in the boiling water, cover and cook for about 8 minutes. Remove with tongs and allow to cool. When cool enough to handle, remove all the meat from the lobsters. Dice the meat and transfer to a medium bowl.

Mix in the mayonnaise, fennel, parsley, chives, chervil, tarragon, lemon juice, and salt and pepper to taste.

Split the éclair buns lengthwise with a bread knife, but not all the way through, leaving a hinge along one side. Divide the lobster mixture among the buns. Stuff each éclair with 2 arugula leaves. Serve.

Cheese

The Terroir of Ontario Cheese

About a hundred years ago, when people had their own dairies, each community would raise dairy cattle and produce cheese. Cheddar was the main cheese produced in Ontario, probably because of people's British roots. There were differences between regions and herds, so the cheddars had different flavour profiles, and this was a good thing. But when pasteurization came along, it changed everything. Pasteurization is a heat treatment process that minimizes microbial activity in fresh milk. While it improved the health of the population overall, pasteurization had a detrimental effect on taste. Once pasteurization became mandated by government, any regional differentiation in taste evaporated. Small cheese companies were bought by the bigger companies, which brought about the decline of small-production, village-based cheese dairies.

These days, we understand a lot more about the safe handling of milk. It's illegal to sell or distribute raw milk in Canada, but we are able to make cheese with raw milk as long as it's aged at least sixty days (to kill off unwanted bacteria) before being sold to the public. Here is what we are finally beginning to learn: when you industrialize things like dairy farming, you lose regional diversity. It's a struggle to bring it back, but we understand, from other jurisdictions that have maintained regional diversity, how beautiful it is, and we are slowly starting to get there.

This is all good news for the evolution of food culture in our society.

MEMORIES OF MILK

My first recollection of milk is its powdered form, during the time of all that post–World War II astronaut-synthesized food. People were so misguided in the '60s with regard to nutrition and processed foods. I think my mum thought it was smart and economical to make powdered milk. I used to plug my nose and close my eyes just so I could have as few sensations associated with that product as possible. I'd have to drink it because otherwise I couldn't leave the table.

So that's my first memory. Eventually my mum just gave up because both my sister and I gave her so much grief about it. I still shudder at the thought of it.

The next thing I remember is milk being delivered by the milkman in glass bottles. Borden Dairy—its logo was a daisy and a cow's face. Still, it was pasteurized, homogenized milk, just regular stuff, no cream rising to the top.

Then I remember when the milkman stopped delivering. When we bought milk at the supermarket, it was in three-quart glass jugs with a plastic handle. I remember you could get 25 cents back on one of those jugs.

Michael Schmidt is a farmer and activist for raw milk. For years he has been waging a war to amend the law to allow consumers to purchase unpasteurized milk. He hasn't been successful yet, but I hope that he will be someday. Of course, people like Michael Schmidt love the taste of raw milk and believe in its health-giving properties, but I think what Michael is advocating for is more than just taste—it is the freedom to choose.

Pickled Vegetables with Niagara Gold Fondue

Makes 6 servings

When I was a young man, I spent one winter working for George Minden and his family in Gstaad, Switzerland. One day George took us to a restaurant that specialized in a dish called *raclette*. It was a snowy evening and the skiers coming off the mountain repaired to this cozy, warm spot to sample the house specialty. The dish is essentially melted and broiled cheese that is scraped off the wheel and served warm and oozing with boiled new potatoes and pickled gherkins and pearl onions. It is customarily enjoyed with a glass or two of a Swiss wine called Fendant. The perfect thing.

You can use any pickled vegetables you have on hand. I am always seeking out new and unusual pickles from the Forbes Wild Foods line of foraged products.

Ingredients

1 jar (1 pint/500 mL) beet-pickled wild leeks (see recipe page 59), drained

1 jar (1 pint/500 mL) pickled cattail hearts or pickled wild mushrooms (see recipe page 289), drained

1 jar (1 pint/500 mL) pickled okra (see recipe page 87), drained

12 ounces (375 g) Niagara Gold or another semi-firm melting cheese

2 tablespoons (30 mL) chopped fresh parsley

¼ cup (60 mL) fine olive oil

Directions

Preheat the oven to 350°F (180°C).

Lay out 6 ovenproof salad plates on a baking sheet. Arrange an assortment of pickled vegetables on each plate. Cut the Niagara Gold into 6 equal slices and drape 1 slice over each of the vegetable arrangements. Place the plates in the oven for approximately 10 minutes or until the cheese has melted nicely over the vegetables. Sprinkle each plate with chopped parsley and a drizzle of olive oil. Serve.

Sheep's Milk Cheese–Filled Squash Flower with Fresh Tomato Sauce

Makes 6 servings

Squash are funny because they don't like to grow in straight rows like beans or radishes but, rather, like a "patch" of their own. When growing zucchini or indeed any squash, you have the added bonus of the drapey, large-petalled flower the plant produces. There is something extra-sensual about preparing dishes involving flowers. Select flowers after they are fully formed, and harvest them in the morning when the petals are closed: it is easier to work with them. Reach inside and pinch off the stamens, leaving room for the filling to follow. These days, even if you don't grow your own zucchini, you can usually find zucchini blossoms in the produce department of specialty grocery stores or at a farmers' market.

Ingredients

3 ounces (90 g) sheep's milk ricotta
   (cow's milk will work as well)
3 fresh basil leaves, roughly chopped
1 celery stalk, finely diced
Pinch of freshly grated nutmeg
Salt and freshly ground black pepper
6 freshly harvested zucchini blossoms,
   stamens removed
3 tablespoons (50 mL) fine olive oil
1 cup (250 mL) J.K. Tomato Sauce (see recipe
   page 133)
2 fresh basil leaves, cut into chiffonade

Directions

Preheat the oven to 325°F (160°C).

Combine the ricotta, chopped basil, celery, nutmeg, and salt and pepper to taste in a small bowl.

Fill the zucchini blossoms with the ricotta mixture. The easiest way to do this is to use a piping bag fitted with a plain tip. Twist the ends of the blossoms to close the "package."

Sprinkle some olive oil on a small baking sheet. Place the filled blossoms on the baking sheet and bake until heated through, about 10 minutes.

Meanwhile, gently reduce the tomato sauce for about 10 minutes.

Lay out 6 salad plates. Spoon about 2 tablespoons (30 mL) of tomato sauce onto each plate. Place a baked zucchini blossom on each plate. Sprinkle with the olive oil and chiffonade of basil. Serve.

253

Cucumber and Sheep's Milk Feta Salad with Bulgur Wheat and Cherry Tomatoes

Makes 4 servings

This is my take on a Greek salad. The earthy bulgur is delicious in combination with the sweet tomatoes, refreshing crunch of cucumbers and the salty, creamy-crumbly feta.

Ingredients

1 cup (250 mL) bulgur

½ cup (125 mL) chopped fresh parsley

¼ cup (60 mL) lemon juice

¼ cup (60 mL) + 2 tablespoons (30 mL) fine olive oil

Salt and freshly ground black pepper

1 cucumber, peeled and cut into large dice

1 red onion, thinly sliced

4 teaspoons (20 mL) red wine vinegar

6 tablespoons (90 mL) crumbled sheep's milk feta

1 tablespoon (15 mL) roughly chopped fresh mint

8 cherry tomatoes, cut in half lengthwise

Directions

Soak the bulgur in cold water for 1 hour. Drain thoroughly. In a medium bowl, mix the bulgur with the parsley, lemon juice and ¼ cup (60 mL) olive oil. Season with salt and pepper.

In a separate bowl, mix together the cucumber, red onion and vinegar. Season with salt and pepper.

Arrange the bulgur mixture in a ring on a serving plate. Spoon the cucumber mixture into the centre. Scatter the feta on top. Sprinkle with the chopped mint and drizzle with 2 tablespoons (30 mL) olive oil. Arrange the cherry tomato halves all around the dish. Serve.

Potato Gnocchi with Thunder Oak Gouda Sauce

Makes 6 servings

Back in 1992 Marcel Réthoré and I reopened Palmerston Restaurant after an eighteen-month hiatus. The new iteration of the restaurant was designed to appeal to our neighbours. To that end we published an à la carte menu as well as a menu that featured dishes that changed each day. Wednesdays were gnocchi with cheese sauce day. I didn't know about Thunder Oak Gouda in those days. I don't think it was being produced yet. Since then our artisanal cheese industry has taken off. I think we owe a debt of gratitude to our Quebec neighbours. Their artisanal cheese industry has been thriving for years. Today a diverse selection of cheeses comes from all over the province. We in Ontario are doing our best to keep up and we now have, in addition to our village cheddar production, a very good selection of cheeses. Thunder Oak Gouda is a Dutch-inspired cheese that hails from Thunder Bay.

Ingredients

Gnocchi

2 pounds (1 kg) russet potatoes (unpeeled)

1 egg, lightly beaten

1 cup (250 mL) all-purpose flour

Salt

Sauce

1 tablespoon (15 mL) butter

1 tablespoon (15 mL) all-purpose flour

1 onion, roughly chopped

1 whole clove

1 bay leaf

2 cups (500 mL) hot milk

Pinch of freshly grated nutmeg

Salt

2½ ounces (75 g) finely grated Thunder
   Oak Gouda

1 tablespoon (15 mL) finely chopped fresh chives

Directions

Preheat the oven to 350°F (180°C).

   For the gnocchi, wrap the potatoes in foil and bake them for 1 hour or until they are soft and yielding to the touch.

Meanwhile, make the sauce. Melt the butter in a small saucepan over medium heat. Add the flour and stir with a wooden spoon until mixed well. Add the onion, clove and bay leaf. Continue to stir over the heat for an additional 5 minutes. Add the hot milk very gradually, stirring constantly until sauce is smooth. Add the nutmeg and simmer the sauce for 10 minutes, stirring from time to time. Season with salt and discard the bay leaf. Remove from the heat and cover the surface with plastic wrap. Reserve at room temperature.

Using a paring knife, peel the potatoes while they are still warm. Place them on a baking sheet and, using the tines of a fork, mash them until evenly broken down. Allow to cool slightly, but while they are still warm, add the egg, most of the flour (reserving some for dusting the work surface) and salt to taste. Use a pastry scraper to fold the ingredients together, forming a crumbly dough.

Divide the dough into 4 pieces. Dust a work surface with the remaining flour and, using your hands, roll 1 piece of dough into a long rope. Using the pastry scraper, cut the rope into 1-inch (2.5 cm) pieces. Repeat with the remaining dough. Gently press the tines of a fork against each gnocchi.

Bring a large pot of water to the boil. Add a generous amount of salt. Cook the gnocchi in batches until they bob to the surface. Transfer them with a slotted spoon to a large serving dish.

Meanwhile, remove the plastic wrap from the sauce and reheat over medium heat. Whisk in most of the grated cheese, reserving some for garnishing the platter. When the cheese is melted, pour the sauce over the gnocchi. Garnish with the remaining grated cheese and the chives. Serve.

Beet and Potato Melt with Cape Vessey Cheese

Makes 4 servings

I kept hearing about Fifth Town Artisan Cheese Company long before the factory was built. Petra Kassun-Mutch had a dream to produce artisanal cheese from goat's and sheep's milk. She and others, like Ruth Klahsen of Monforte Dairy in Stratford, are helping to reshape the artisanal cheese industry in Ontario. Petra and I worked together to develop this recipe. I wanted a cheese with good melting properties, and she suggested her Cape Vessey, a firm goat's milk cheese. It worked beautifully.

Ingredients

8 fingerling potatoes

4 candy-cane beets or other heirloom variety

Juice from 3 raw beets

4 ounces (125 g) Cape Vessey or other firm goat's milk cheese

2 shallots, finely chopped and soaked in cider vinegar

1 green onion, thinly sliced on the bias

Directions

Cook the potatoes and beets in separate pots of boiling water until tender. In a third pot, gently simmer the beet juice until reduced to a syrup.

Drain the potatoes and beets and let them air dry. While they are still warm, peel the beets and cut them into thin rounds. Cross-hatch the potatoes with a paring knife and smoosh them between your thumb and index finger as you would a baked potato.

Cut the cheese into 4 long slices. Place the beet slices in a slightly overlapping circle on 4 oven-proof plates. Place 2 smooshed potatoes on top of the beets. Top with the sliced cheese. Place each plate under the broiler until the cheese is melted and golden. Drain the shallots, then sprinkle the shallots and sliced green onions over each plate. Spoon some reduced beet juice onto each plate and serve immediately.

Blintzes with Sheep's Milk Ricotta

Makes 6 servings

Eric Savics and I signed the lease for Palmerston Restaurant in March 1985. There was much to do to get ready for our opening on June 17. We all broke for lunch at noon or one o'clock every day. Sometimes we packed a lunch, sometimes we would go to Mars Diner just a few blocks away on College Street. We got to know their daily specials. They would have them on a seven-day rotation. (That may have inspired our later habit of a weekly roster of changing daily specials at Palmerston.) Tuesday was cabbage rolls, Wednesday meatloaf, Thursday cheese blintzes. I would watch the old-timers ordering the blintzes. The waitresses always offered applesauce or sour cream on the side. "Gimme both," said one man. The waitress obliged and brought him a small ramekin brimming with both. I tried the same trick and thought "how clever!"

Ingredients

2 medium apples (any kind), peeled, cored
    and chopped
1 cup (250 mL) sweet apple cider
Crêpe batter (see recipe page 52) using sifted
    pastry flour in place of wild rice flour
1 egg
½ cup (100 g) granulated sugar
1⅔ cups (400 mL) sheep's milk ricotta
½ teaspoon (2 mL) vanilla extract
Zest of 1 lemon

¼ cup (60 mL) butter
6 tablespoons (90 mL) sour cream

Directions

Place the cut apples and cider in a small saucepan. Bring to the boil, then reduce heat to low and cook until the apples are tender and falling apart. Remove from the heat and cool to room temperature.

Meanwhile, using one or more small nonstick crêpe pans, make 12 crêpes about 4 inches (10 cm) in diameter.

In a medium bowl, beat together the egg and sugar with a whisk until light and fluffy. Add the ricotta, vanilla and lemon zest and mix well.

Lay out the crêpes on the counter. Top each with about 2 tablespoons (30 mL) ricotta mixture. Fold the bottom of the crêpe over the filling, then fold in the sides. Roll up the crêpe, completely enclosing the filling.

In a large frying pan, melt the butter and gently fry the blintzes until golden brown on both sides.

Lay out 6 plates. Serve 2 blintzes per person. Place bowls of sour cream and the cooked apples on the table with the blintzes.

259

THE CHEESE PLATE

During the span of my career the quality of Ontario cheese production has increased by leaps and bounds. We still include some excellent artisanal cheeses from Quebec on the cheese plates at our restaurant, but we could easily create a beautiful selection solely from Ontario dairies. To assemble an impressive cheese plate, include some goat's and sheep's milk cheeses along with cow's milk varieties. As well, aim to include a washed-rind cheese, a bloomy-rind cheese, a blue and a cheddar. Some accoutrements that we include on our cheese plate are quince jelly (see recipe page 285), toasted walnuts and, always, wild rice crackers (see recipe page 263).

Wild Rice Crackers

Makes approximately 100 crackers

Ingredients

6 cups (660 g) hard flour

1½ cups (225 g) wild rice flour

3 tablespoons (50 mL) granulated sugar

¼ teaspoon (1 mL) salt, plus extra for sprinkling

2 cups + 2 tablespoons (510 g) cold butter, cubed

2½ cups (625 mL) buttermilk, plus extra as needed

1 egg white, lightly beaten

Directions

Combine the flour, wild rice flour, sugar and ¼ teaspoon (1 mL) salt in a large bowl. Add the butter and cut in until the mixture resembles coarse meal. Add the buttermilk and stir just until the mixture comes together. (You may need a little more buttermilk.) Do not over-mix. Gather dough into a ball, flatten into a disc, wrap in plastic wrap and chill for 1 hour.

Preheat the oven to 325°F (160°C). Line a baking sheet with parchment paper or a nonstick baking mat.

On a lightly floured surface, roll out the dough to ⅛-inch (3 mm) thickness. Transfer rolled dough to the baking sheet. Prick all over with a fork. Use a pizza cutter to score dough into 3-inch (7.5 cm) triangles. Brush with egg white and sprinkle with salt.

Bake until golden brown, 8 to 10 minutes. Cool on racks. When cool, snap into individual crackers. Store in an airtight container for up to 2 weeks.

Soup

Soup and Politics

Soupstock was the result of the desire to protest a massive quarry of unprecedented size being planned for the middle of prime farmland, and a pivotal watershed, in central Ontario. My great friend Chef Michael Stadtländer organized it in 2012, one year after his successful Foodstock protest. He wanted Soupstock to be bigger, and it was. Organized in collaboration with the Canadian Chefs' Congress and the David Suzuki Foundation, over two hundred chefs from across Canada and the U.S. gathered. We made soup in peaceful protest of the proposed mega-quarry. To our amazement, about forty thousand people showed up. Jim Cuddy of Blue Rodeo and Snowblink were among the performers, and George Stroumboulopoulos was the emcee. It was a huge spectacle, with tens of thousands of people eating soup in the sunshine, and it forced the Ontario government to take notice. It put a halt to the quarry long enough to do an environmental assessment. Shortly after Soupstock, ceding to the overwhelming opposition to the proposal, Highland Companies withdrew its application to develop the quarry.

2011's Foodstock and 2012's Soupstock are the largest culinary events/protests in world history.

Swiss Chard Soup

Makes 6 servings

I admire Michael Stadtländer for taking the lead in the important mega-quarry protest. It's incredible how powerful a coalition of people from the food service industry, the agricultural sector and the general public can be, prevailing against seemingly insurmountable big-business and big-government odds.

That summer I had a bumper crop of Swiss chard on my farm. It was clear what I would use to make two thousand portions of soup. In case you're not looking to make that many portions, here is a scaled-down version of the recipe.

Ingredients

12 Swiss chard leaves
¼ cup (60 mL) sunflower oil
2 medium onions, thinly sliced
3 cloves garlic, thinly sliced
1 green chili, very finely chopped
3 medium Yukon Gold potatoes, peeled
   (2 thinly sliced and 1 finely diced)
12 cups (3 L) vegetable stock
¼ cup (60 g) butter
2 shallots, finely chopped
Salt and freshly ground black pepper

Directions

Cut the centre rib and stem from each chard leaf and finely chop the stems. Reserve the leaves and stems separately.

In a large soup pot over medium heat, combine the sunflower oil, onions, garlic, chili and chard leaves, stirring from time to time until the chard has totally wilted, approximately 10 minutes. Add the sliced potatoes and vegetable stock. Bring to the boil, then reduce heat and simmer for about 20 minutes.

In a blender or food processor, purée the soup in batches. Return to the pot.

In a small saucepan over medium heat, combine the butter, shallots and chard stems. Gently sauté for about 5 minutes. Add the diced potato and season with salt and pepper. Cover, reduce heat to low and simmer for about 10 minutes or until potatoes are tender.

Meanwhile, bring the soup back to the boil.

Lay out 6 soup bowls. Add a dollop of the chard stem mixture to each bowl. Fill each bowl with soup. Serve.

Sunchoke Soup with Chips

Makes 4 servings

Sunchokes, also known as Jerusalem artichokes, grow abundantly in Southern Ontario. They are a part of the sunflower family but are cultivated for their rhizomes. I have even heard of these rhizomes being distilled to fuel farm machinery. When roasted and puréed, sunchokes have a rich, earthy flavour, reminiscent of toasted sunflower seeds.

You can skip the chips if you prefer. A drizzle of herb-infused oil makes a pretty garnish.

Ingredients

⅓ cup (80 g) butter
1 medium onion, finely chopped
10 ounces (300 g) sunchokes, peeled and chopped
4 cups (1 L) strong chicken stock
Salt and freshly ground black pepper
2 cups (500 mL) sunflower oil
1 sunchoke, peeled and thinly sliced

Directions

Warm the butter and onion in a large soup pot. Stir in the chopped sunchokes and gently sauté for 10 minutes. Add the chicken stock. Bring to the boil, then reduce heat and simmer for 30 minutes. Season with salt and pepper.

Meanwhile, heat the sunflower oil in a medium saucepan to 275°F (140°C). Gently fry the sliced sunchoke until golden brown. Drain on paper towels. Sprinkle with salt.

Purée the soup in a blender until very smooth. Pour soup into 4 soup bowls. Garnish each serving with the fried sunchoke chips. Serve.

Curried Baked Squash Soup

Makes 6 servings

There have been several iterations of this soup over the years. Baked squash seems to evoke images of fall and the cooler weather. It glows in the pot like a fire in the hearth.

I love to serve this soup with a bit of crème fraîche and a garnish of squash chips.

Ingredients

2 cloves garlic, minced

1 tablespoon (15 mL) finely chopped peeled fresh ginger

½ teaspoon (2 mL) ground cardamom

½ teaspoon (2 mL) freshly grated nutmeg

1 green chili, very finely chopped

¼ cup (60 g) butter

1 buttercup squash, split in half lengthwise, seeds and membrane removed

8 cups (2 L) vegetable stock

Salt and freshly ground black pepper

Directions

Preheat the oven to 375°F (190°C).

Divide the garlic, ginger, cardamom, nutmeg, chili and butter between the cavities of the squash halves. Place the squash halves cut side up on a baking sheet and cover loosely with foil. Bake for approximately 1 hour or until squash is soft to the touch. Let the squash cool until you can handle it without burning yourself.

Scrape the squash from its skin and transfer to a soup pot. Discard the skin. Add the vegetable stock. Bring to the boil, then reduce heat and simmer for about 15 minutes, stirring from time to time. Using an immersion blender or a standard blender, purée the soup. Season with salt and pepper. Ladle into 6 bowls and serve.

Roasted Carrot Soup

Makes 6 servings

I was once in a restaurant in Brooklyn, and roasted carrot was on the menu. I ordered it, curious to see how it would be presented. I received a whole carrot, properly cooked and not much else. When I cut into it, it released a perfume so redolent of the essence of carrot, all I could do was smile contentedly and enjoy every last morsel. Start with a beautifully grown organic carrot, roast it as opposed to boiling it and don't muddle the essence of it with added ingredients. Find carrots that were grown locally. This soup reflects that approach. Pictured here, the carrot soup is served half and half with Sunchoke Soup with Chips (see recipe page 269).

Ingredients

1¼ cups (300 mL) sunflower oil
6 medium carrots, scrubbed (1 sliced as thinly as
    possible with a mandoline)
1 onion, finely chopped
Salt
2 shallots, finely chopped
¼ cup (60 g) butter
8 cups (2 L) vegetable stock
Crème fraîche, to serve

Directions

Preheat the oven to 300°F (150°C).

Pour ¼ cup (60 mL) of the sunflower oil into a large ovenproof saucepan or roasting pan that has a tight-fitting lid. Add the 5 whole carrots and the onion. Cover and roast for about 1 hour or until the carrots are soft.

Meanwhile, in a small saucepan, heat the remaining 1 cup (250 mL) sunflower oil to 300°F (150°C). Fry the carrot slices a few at a time in the hot oil, stirring with a slotted spoon to ensure an even doneness. The carrot "chips" should darken to a golden orange—not too dark—when they are done. Drain on paper towels and let cool. Sprinkle lightly with salt. Reserve.

Once the carrots are finished roasting, dice 1 carrot and place it in a small ovenproof saucepan with the shallots and butter. Cover and roast in the oven for 20 minutes.

Meanwhile, bring the vegetable stock to the boiling point. Cut the remaining 4 roasted carrots into chunks that will fit in a blender. In two or three batches, purée the carrot pieces with the hot vegetable stock. Transfer the soup to a saucepan and heat to serving temperature. Season with salt.

Lay out 6 bowls. Place a spoonful of diced carrot-shallot mixture in each bowl. Pour the soup on top. Garnish with a few carrot chips and a drizzle of crème fraîche, if you like. Serve.

Roasted Pumpkin Soup with Sunchoke

Makes 6 servings

I remember as a George Brown student in Toronto, wandering through Kensington Market. This was when the culinary department was housed in an old warehouse building on Nassau Street. The school occupied the third and fourth floors. The world inside was so different from the world down below. Portuguese, South American and West Indian hawkers populated the stalls selling ingredients rarely seen in the temple to French gastronomy upstairs. But as a cook I needed to pay attention to what was going on around me. This meant, because I lived in Toronto, being open to the traditions of cooking from many parts of the world. Kensington Market was a microcosm of what a multicultural place Toronto is. Upstairs at George Brown and in the kitchen of the Windsor Arms Hotel, I was learning a language and a set of skills that was specific to French cuisine, but that tool kit eventually enabled me to allow other cuisines and culinary traditions to inspire my approach to cooking.

I was used to the pumpkins we see in North America for Halloween—the ones that are wonderful to carve into jack-o'-lanterns and illuminate with a candle, but rather insipid tasting. It was during one of my walks in Kensington that I spied a different sort of pumpkin that was being sold in wedges still glistening from the knife's incision. The meat looked more firm and deeper in colour, with a green mottled exterior. "In Jamaica we use these for making soup," said the man at the stall. "Bake them with ginger and allspice first." To complement the deep, rich taste of the pumpkin, I have added a purée of sunchoke to swirl in at the last moment.

Ingredients

1 Jamaican pumpkin or acorn squash (3 pounds/ 1.5 kg)

2 tablespoons (30 mL) finely chopped peeled fresh ginger

1 teaspoon (5 mL) ground allspice

¼ cup (60 mL) water

12 cups (3 L) vegetable stock

Salt and freshly ground black pepper

¼ cup (60 g) butter

1 pound (500 g) sunchokes (Jerusalem artichokes), peeled and chopped

1 medium onion, finely chopped

Directions

Preheat the oven to 350°F (180°C). Cut up the pumpkin into 2-inch (5 cm) chunks and place them in a baking dish. Sprinkle with the ginger and allspice. Add the water, cover tightly with foil and bake for 1 hour or until the pumpkin is tender.

274

When the pumpkin is cool enough to handle, use
a paring knife to separate the flesh from the skin.
Discard the skin. Transfer the flesh and any liquid
in the baking dish to a soup pot. Add the vegetable stock and bring to the boil. Reduce heat and
simmer for 15 minutes.

Transfer the soup in batches to a blender or food
processor and purée. Return to the pot, season with
salt and pepper, and reserve.

In a small saucepan with a tight-fitting lid, combine the butter, sunchokes and onion. Cover and
simmer over low heat, stirring from time to time,
until the sunchoke is very tender, approximately
30 minutes. Transfer to a clean blender and blend
until smooth.

Bring the pumpkin soup back to the boiling
point. Lay out 6 bowls and pour soup into each
bowl. Add a dollop of sunchoke purée to each bowl
and use a teaspoon to swirl the purée through the
soup in a pleasing pattern. Serve.

Minestrone with Braised Rabbit

Makes 6 servings

This is a time of accelerated evolution as cooks and growers all over the world are realizing the importance and beauty of examining and practising their craft through the local context. This process of teasing out excellence and uniqueness in the regions is giving rise to a new sense of validation in our work. Much has been accomplished towards this end in the last decade, and much more work in knitting together local networks of supply and representation will continue to happen. A couple of years ago I was asked to consult on a new restaurant, Windows by Jamie Kennedy, in Niagara Falls, Ontario. This was an opportunity to share operating philosophies and cooking practices with a team of people from the Niagara region. I have been grateful for the support shown by Canadian Niagara Hotels to bring local procurement practices to the Falls. Ross Midgley, the chef of the restaurant, and I have collaborated to bring about a new dining experience for visitors to the Falls, one that genuinely represents the region where this natural wonder of the world is situated.

One event that Ross and I worked on together featured this soup. Diners sat at a long table mesmerized by the clear view of the Falls, the force of nature just outside the window, and were comforted by the soothing taste of this minestrone.

Ingredients

Broth

1 whole rabbit

12 cups (3 L) chicken stock

2 medium onions, roughly chopped

2 celery stalks, roughly chopped

2 medium carrots, roughly chopped

3 bay leaves

3 whole cloves

12 black peppercorns

1 large sprig of fresh thyme

Soup

½ cup (125 mL) dried white beans, soaked overnight and drained

1 leek, thinly sliced

1 carrot, diced

1 celery stalk, diced

Pesto

2 tablespoons (30 mL) grated hard sheep's milk cheese such as Toscano from Monforte

2 tablespoons (30 mL) fresh basil leaves

1 tablespoon (15 mL) toasted walnut halves

¼ cup (60 mL) cold-pressed sunflower oil

recipe continues . . .

Directions

To make the broth, place the rabbit in a large soup pot and cover with the chicken stock. Add the onions, celery, carrots, bay leaves, cloves, peppercorns and thyme. Add enough cold water to cover. Bring to the boil. Reduce heat and simmer for 2 hours or until the rabbit meat falls away from the bone.

Meanwhile, in a small saucepan, cook the beans, generously covered with water, for about 45 minutes or until tender. Drain and reserve.

Remove the rabbit from the pot and cool at room temperature. Strain the rich cooking broth and reserve. Discard the vegetables.

When the rabbit is cool enough to handle, pick all the meat from the bones, discarding the bones. Return all the meat to the soup pot and add the leek, carrot, celery, cooked beans and rabbit broth. Bring to the boil, then reduce heat and simmer for 20 minutes.

Meanwhile, make the pesto. Put the cheese, basil leaves, walnuts and oil in a food processor and purée.

Lay out 6 bowls. Ladle soup into the bowls. Top each serving with a dollop of pesto. Serve.

Above: Ross Midgley

Moroccan Spiced Vegetable Soup

Makes 10 servings

Many years ago I spent time in Paris with a group of Moroccan friends. I have happy memories of sitting around on the floor sharing from a central platter of food and eating with our hands. This style of eating is the ultimate example of dining as a communal act. This recipe comprises the flavour combinations I remember most from that time in my life.

Ingredients

¼ cup (60 mL) olive oil

1 tablespoon (15 mL) minced garlic

1 pound (500 g) onions, finely chopped

2 tablespoons (30 mL) ground cumin

2 tablespoons (30 mL) sweet paprika

1 teaspoon (5 mL) Hungarian hot paprika

1 can (28 ounces/796 mL) diced tomatoes

8 cups (2 L) vegetable stock

¾ cup (175 mL) finely diced carrot

3 cups (750 mL) finely diced butternut squash

2 cups (500 mL) finely diced peeled sweet potato

1 cup (250 mL) finely diced zucchini

¾ cup (175 mL) finely diced leek

¾ cup (175 mL) finely diced celery

2 bay leaves

½ teaspoon (2 mL) salt

3 tablespoons (50 mL) chopped fresh coriander
(optional)

Directions

Warm the olive oil in a soup pot. Add the garlic and onions and simmer for 5 minutes. Stir in the cumin, sweet paprika and hot paprika. Add the diced tomatoes and vegetable stock; bring to the boil. Add the carrot, squash, sweet potato, zucchini, leek, celery, bay leaves and salt. Cook over medium heat until vegetables are tender, approximately 15 minutes. Discard the bay leaves. Serve garnished with chopped fresh coriander, if desired.

Preserves

My three great-aunts, Olive, Myrtle and May, all lived together in a house that their father built in Davisville, a neighbourhood of Toronto. They lived in that house their whole lives. They were spiritual women, charter members of Manor Road United Church. I remember going into their basement and seeing shelves full of preserves, in those old glass jars with broad zinc bands holding on the thick glass lids. The basement was filled with their pickles and jams, beets, dills and green beans. The mustard pickle I use at the restaurant is Aunt Myrtle's recipe. I started interviewing her about the process when I was seventeen, after I'd begun my apprenticeship. She was surprised but delighted at my interest in a tradition normally associated with the women in the family. It was most unusual for a man to care about that kind of thing, apart from enjoying it at the table. My wanting to know the recipes and the whole culture behind it was kind of a shock to all of them.

Canning and preserving, to me, is one of the culinary traditions of living in Southern Ontario. Once upon a time we needed to preserve to get through the winter. It was a natural way of handling a season's abundance, and it became a cultural component of life in Southern Ontario, which gives us something in common with the folks in Bangor, Maine, but sets us apart from, say, Miami, Florida.

Preserving is a time-consuming thing. It's a full-time endeavour that doesn't stop until all the harvest is in.

Our company represented the province of Ontario at the Canadian Chefs' Congress in 2012, and I felt it would be great to present a "heritage Ontario pantry." I found all these old jars, thick glass just like my great-aunts used to use, and then I researched old Ontario recipes. We picked walnuts, green and in the shell, and pickled them; we pickled beets with cloves; we pickled eggs with ginger. Ken Steele and I drove to the East Coast in a van filled to the roof with these jars, to serve our dish at the congress.

Nowadays I grow a lot of drying tomatoes, the small cherry-sized tomatoes. We dry them before curing them in oil and salt. They don't come out dried and leathery, because they still have a bit of juice. It's almost as though part of the day's sunshine and the temperature goes into the jar with them.

The tomatoes are consistently amazing. I can expect to preserve about thirty bushels by the end of the season. Typically we do about two hundred jars of tomato sauce, two hundred jars of dill pickles and three hundred of mustard pickle. People are crazy for Aunt Myrtle's mustard pickle—we use it on everything.

Some of the apprentices have no experience preserving, so they are kind of wide-eyed when they see us pickling things like hard-boiled eggs and green walnuts still in their shells. They're just like I was in my great-aunts' basement. We teach them the process just like Olive, Myrtle and May taught me. They see the shelves in the dining room filled with jars of everything we've canned from the summer. Then, when winter comes, they see that we are taking these jars down from the shelves and actually using them. They aren't just for decor—we're actually embracing this old-school philosophy.

CANNING BASICS

Canning is a safe method for preserving food. The process involves placing foods in jars and heating them to a temperature that destroys micro-organisms that cause food to spoil. As the jars are heated, some air is forced out, and as the jars cool, the air inside shrinks, creating a vacuum seal that prevents air (and any micro-organisms it might contain) from getting into the jar. Properly canned foods will last stored in a cool, dry environment for up to a year if unopened. Once opened, refrigerate.

Although there are many techniques for canning, we use only one approach in this book. All the canning recipes use the boiling-water bath method.

Equipment

Here is a list of equipment to have on hand when you are preparing one of my recipes:
- appropriately sized mason jars (each recipe specifies the size of jar to use)
- new self-sealing "snap" lids
- screw-top metal band to secure the self-sealing lids in place
- a large pot deep enough to hold your jars completely submerged under water, and fitted with a rack to prevent jars from bumping into each other
- a jar lifter (helpful for removing jars from hot water)
- a canning funnel (helpful for cleanly guiding ingredients into jars)

Sterilizing Equipment

• Preheat the oven to 275°F (140°C). Place the jars on the oven rack and heat them for 30 minutes. Carefully remove the jars and set them upright on the counter.

• Place the self-sealing lids (but not the screw bands) in a pot of water and bring just to the boil. Turn off the heat and leave the lids in the hot water until needed. This will soften the sealing compound on the inside of the lid.

Processing

• Leave headspace to allow for air to expand and contract. If pickling vegetables or preserving fruits, fill the jars to 1/2 inch (1 cm) from the brim. If making jams or jellies, fill the jars to 1/4 inch (5 mm) from the brim.

• Wipe the rims with a clean cloth and place the self-sealing lid on top. Screw on the metal band just until fingertip-tight.

• Place the jars in the pot of water and bring to a boil (rather than placing the jars in boiling water). Process for the length of time stated in the recipe.

• Jars should not touch each other while in the pot.

• After the jars have cooled, test for a proper seal: the lid should be slightly concave. If it is flat or convex, the seal has been compromised. Keep the jar refrigerated and consume within a couple of weeks.

• Jars and screw bands may be reused, but always use new self-sealing lids.

Quince Jelly

Makes six 1-pint (500 mL) jars

Quince is a fruit that is native to Asia and the Mediterranean and is related to the apple family. Many cultures make a kind of sweet paste from it for enjoying on toast or as an accompaniment to cheese. When picked ripe it is extremely aromatic, reminiscent of a tropical fruit or flower. It must be cooked, however, as it is extremely woody and not pleasant to eat uncooked. I was delighted to discover that the fruit grows in our climate and is available in the fall.

Ingredients

11 pounds (5 kg) fresh ripe quince
7 fluid ounces (200 mL) water
5 pounds (2.5 kg) fine granulated sugar
½ cup (125 mL) liquid pectin

Directions

For canning instructions, see pages 282–83.

Cut quince into small pieces. Place the quince and the water in a large pot. Bring to the boil. Reduce heat, cover and simmer for approximately 20 minutes or until quince is very soft.

Suspend a colander lined with cheesecloth over another large pot. Transfer the cooked quince and any cooking liquid to the colander. Let drain overnight in the refrigerator.

Discard the solids and measure 12 cups (3 L) of the quince liquid. Add the sugar and boil vigorously for 10 minutes, skimming from time to time. Add the liquid pectin and boil for an additional 3 minutes.

Pour jelly into 6 sterilized 1-pint (500 mL) mason jars, leaving ¼-inch (5 mm) headspace. Seal jars and process in boiling water for 15 minutes. Cool on the counter and store in a cool, dark place.

Preserved Summer Fruits in Syrup

Makes four 1-pint (500 mL) jars

The season of summer fruits is so fleeting that we are compelled to can as much of it as possible before the leaves turn.

Ingredients

1 cup (200 g) granulated sugar

1 cup (250 mL) water

1 lemon, sliced

5 pounds (2.2 kg) pitted plum halves, pitted and peeled peach halves or any ripe, sound summer stone fruit

Directions

For canning instructions, see pages 282–83.

In a saucepan, boil the sugar, water and lemon rapidly for 20 minutes. Pack fruit into 4 sterilized 1-pint (500 mL) jars. Remove lemon slices from syrup and pour syrup over fruit, covering all the fruit but leaving ½-inch (1 cm) headspace. Seal jars and process in boiling water for 20 minutes. Cool on the counter and store in a cool, dark place.

Pickling Brine

Makes 20 cups (5 L)

We use this multipurpose brine solution for many of our savoury pickles, from beans to carrots to cauliflower to roasted red peppers. It is a basic medium to which we add spices and flavourings that suit what we're pickling.

Ingredients

16 cups (4 L) vegetable stock or water

6 cups (1.5 L) white vinegar

½ cup (100 g) granulated sugar

6 tablespoons (90 mL) black peppercorns

⅓ cup (75 mL) mustard seeds

⅓ cup (75 mL) fine sea salt

3 bay leaves

3 whole cloves

Directions

Combine all the ingredients in a stock pot. Bring to the boil. Reduce heat and simmer for 10 minutes. Strain. Store in a plastic bucket with a tight-fitting lid in a cool, dark place for up to 3 months.

Pickled Wild Mushrooms

Make four 1-pint (500 mL) jars

These make a wonderful accompaniment to a charcuterie board.

Ingredients

5 pounds (2.2 kg) wild or oyster mushrooms
4 sprigs of fresh thyme
4 cups (1 L) pickling brine (see recipe page 287)

Directions

For canning instructions, see pages 282–83.

Brush any visible dirt from the mushrooms and trim the stems. Lightly pack into 4 sterilized 1-pint (500 mL) mason jars to maximum capacity but without crushing the mushrooms. Place 1 sprig of thyme in each jar. Fill jars to just below the rim with the pickling brine. Seal jars and process in boiling water for 20 minutes. Cool on the counter and store in a cool, dark place.

Dill Pickles

Makes four 1-quart (1 L) jars

I wish this recipe would be taught to kids in grade school. Everyone should know how to make their own dill pickles. This is the way my great-aunts made theirs, and I've yet to improve upon it, although I do give the option of adding some heat with serrano chilies.

Ingredients

4 pounds (2 kg) pickling cucumbers

4 cups (1 L) white vinegar

4 cups (1 L) water

½ cup (100 g) granulated sugar

4 teaspoons (20 g) salt

4 large stems of fresh flowering pickling dill

4 teaspoons (20 mL) mustard seeds

2 teaspoons (10 mL) black peppercorns

8 whole cloves

8 cloves garlic, peeled

4 green serrano chilies (optional)

Directions

For canning instructions, see pages 282–83.

Scrub the cucumbers well, place in a tub of ice water and refrigerate overnight.

Combine the vinegar, water, sugar and salt in a large pot and boil for several minutes to dissolve the sugar. Set this pickling brine aside to cool.

Drain the cucumbers. Into each of 4 sterilized 1-quart (1 L) mason jars, place 1 stem of flowering pickling dill, 1 teaspoon (5 mL) mustard seeds, ½ teaspoon (2 mL) black peppercorns, 2 whole cloves, 2 garlic cloves cut into quarters, and 1 green serrano chili, if desired. Fill each jar with cucumbers, and fill with the pickling brine, leaving ½-inch (1 cm) headspace. Seal jars and process in boiling water for 20 minutes. Cool on the counter and store in a cool, dark place.

Raspberry Vinegar

Makes 4 cups (1 L)

When it gets hot and humid during the summer in Southern Ontario, I like to offer refreshing drinks with a hint of fruit flavour, acidity and sweetness. Because I try to use local ingredients, in this recipe I replace the citric acid from lemons or oranges with acetic acid from cider vinegar. There is wonderful fruit flavour from the raspberries and the rich organoleptic sweetness of honey rather than cane sugar.

Ingredients

3 cups (750 mL) freshly picked raspberries
3 cups (750 mL) water
⅔ cup (150 mL) cider vinegar
7 tablespoons (100 mL) honey

Directions

Place all the ingredients in a large nonreactive bowl. Break up the raspberries with a whisk and let the mixture macerate, covered and refrigerated, overnight.

Line a colander with several layers of cheesecloth and suspend it over a nonreactive bowl. Transfer the raspberry mixture to the colander. Let drain overnight in the refrigerator.

Transfer vinegar to a clean jar or bottle. Vinegar will keep, refrigerated, for many months.

To use, pour ¼ cup to 6 tablespoons (60 to 90 mL) of the raspberry vinegar into a tall glass. Add a couple of ice cubes and fill the glass with still or sparkling water. Garnish with a sprig of mint.

Roasted Red Peppers

Makes eight 1-pint (500 mL) jars

I had set up a little charcoal-burning barbecue in my backyard in the High Park neighbourhood. It was autumn and Julia was just a baby. The light was soft and there was a vague scent of burning leaves in the air. I lit the barbecue and settled myself with Julia and a bushel of red peppers to enjoy the afternoon sun.

Ingredients

30 pounds (14 kg) ripe red bell peppers
1 bunch of fresh Greek oregano
12 cups (3 L) pickling brine (see recipe page 287)

Directions

For canning instructions, see pages 282–83.

Light a charcoal barbecue (or heat a propane one). Let the embers reach an even heat. Fill the grilling rack with peppers. When the skin blackens, turn the peppers. Keep doing this until the peppers are evenly charred all around. Place charred peppers in a large bowl and cover. Repeat with remaining peppers.

When peppers are cool enough to handle, remove the charred skin and all the seeds. Pack peppers into 8 sterilized 1-pint (500 mL) mason jars. Put a sprig of oregano in each jar. Fill each jar with pickling brine, leaving ½-inch (1 cm) headspace. Seal jars and process in boiling water for 15 minutes. Cool on the counter and store in a cool, dark place.

Aunt Myrtle's Mustard Pickle

Makes twelve 1-pint (500 mL) jars

In my great-aunts' house, weekend lunches featured sliced leftover meats from dinners during the week. Right there beside the cold roast beef was always a bowl of mustard pickle. The combination is heavenly.

Ingredients

1 pound (500 g) cucumbers, roughly chopped
1 pound (500 g) onions, roughly chopped
1 pound (500 g) green tomatoes, roughly chopped
½ small green cabbage, roughly chopped
½ small cauliflower, roughly chopped
1 green bell pepper, roughly chopped
1 red bell pepper, roughly chopped
3 tablespoons (50 mL) salt
1¼ cups (250 g) granulated sugar
¾ cup (90 g) all-purpose flour
2 tablespoons (30 mL) dry mustard
1 teaspoon (5 mL) turmeric
½ teaspoon (2 mL) celery seeds
½ teaspoon (2 mL) mustard seeds
2½ cups (625 mL) white vinegar

Directions

For canning instructions, see pages 282–83.

Place batches of the vegetables in a food processor and pulse to chop until vegetables achieve a coarse texture. Place chopped vegetables in a large pot and toss with the salt. Cover with boiling water and let stand for 1 hour. Drain thoroughly.

Meanwhile, in a medium bowl, mix the sugar, flour, dry mustard, turmeric, celery seeds and mustard seeds. Whisk in ½ cup (125 mL) of the white vinegar to make a paste.

Bring the remaining 2 cups (500 mL) vinegar to the boil in a large saucepan. Stirring continuously, slowly add the mustard paste, stirring until everything is incorporated. Add all the vegetables and slowly return to the boil.

Transfer to 12 sterilized 1-pint (500 mL) mason jars, leaving ½-inch (1 cm) headspace. Seal jars and process in boiling water for 15 minutes. Cool on the counter and store in a cool, dark place.

Beer-Braised Meat Pie with Mustard Pickle

Makes 6 servings

I love meat pie. I love it hot. I love it cold. Either way, I love it more with mustard pickle.

Ingredients

½ cup (125 mL) sunflower oil

1¼ pounds (625 g) outside round of beef, cut into large cubes

All-purpose flour for dredging

1¼ pounds (625 g) onions, finely chopped

8 ounces (250 g) finely diced carrots

8 ounces (250 g) finely diced celery

8 ounces (250 g) finely chopped leeks

3½ ounces (100 g) thinly sliced garlic

6 tablespoons (90 mL) tomato paste

2 bottles (12 fluid ounces/341 mL each) local craft beer

1½ cups (375 mL) beef stock

1 bay leaf

1 tablespoon (15 mL) chopped fresh thyme

Salt and freshly ground black pepper

Pastry for double-crust 10-inch (25 cm) pie (use your favourite recipe)

Egg wash (1 egg beaten with 1 teaspoon/5 mL water)

Aunt Myrtle's Mustard Pickle (see recipe page 294), to serve

Directions

Heat the sunflower oil in a large flameproof casserole dish over high heat. Working in batches, dredge cubes of beef in the flour and sear them in the hot oil. Remove beef from the casserole and reserve. Reduce heat to medium and add the onions, carrots, celery, leeks and garlic; gently sauté for 5 minutes, stirring from time to time.

Stir in the tomato paste and continue to sauté until the tomato paste is browned nicely. Add the local craft beer, beef stock, bay leaf and thyme. Bring to the boil, then reduce heat to a simmer. Season with salt and pepper. Add the seared beef cubes and any accumulated juices, cover and braise until beef is tender but not falling apart, approximately 2 hours. Cool to room temperature in the pot before placing in the refrigerator to chill overnight.

The next day, preheat the oven to 350°F (180°C). Remove the bay leaf from the meat filling.

Roll out half of the pastry and line a 10-inch (25 cm) pie plate. Fill the pie shell with the meat filling. Roll out the remaining pastry and cover the pie, crimping the edges to seal. Brush with the egg wash and cut 3 slits in the top crust.

Bake for approximately 1 hour or until pastry is golden brown. Serve hot or cold with mustard pickle or chili sauce.

winter

WINTER IS A TIME FOR BOLD FLAVOURS, HEARTY

MEATS, ROBUST ROOT VEGETABLES, THICK-CUT

SLICES OF HOMEMADE BREAD AND EXOTIC SPICES

TO WAKE YOU UP AND PUT SOME FIRE IN YOUR

CHILLED BONES. THIS IS WHEN WE CAN ENJOY

THE JARS OF PRESERVES PUT AWAY FROM THE

HARVEST. THIS IS WHEN WE LET THINGS COOK,

LOW AND SLOW, LONG BRAISES WHILE

THE SNOW FALLS OUTSIDE.

Gilead

We have swept and mopped after service night in the wine bar. The water on the floor has barely enough time to dry before Scott comes in at six a.m. to begin baking. Gilead is like many restaurants are: all about execution and renewal. Barely a sentence or two is spoken about the previous day before we are all consumed with today. We evaluate yesterday, almost subconsciously, to perhaps improve upon what we offer today in food, service and ambience.

At Gilead, we are open for breakfast, lunch and dinner. The light in the room changes dramatically as the day wears on. I love how we shift from service to service, applying changes to the room and adding items to the menu that reflect the desires of our customers. We serve regular customers at every service. Sometimes our customers come for breakfast, lunch and dinner, all on the same day. I think the feeling in the restaurant, that feeling of community, is what continues to fascinate me and keeps me in the game. It is not a job. It is a way of life.

I remember a wedding I catered years ago at St. Lawrence Hall. On the main floor of the building was a restaurant. I noticed a man observing our arrival and the subsequent activity in the hall. I determined that he must work in the restaurant. I struck up a conversation with him and felt a connection that compelled me to offer him a job with my organization. This man was Thayalan Thambithurai, a.k.a. Seeva. More than twenty years later he is the stalwart, loyal employee whose character I sensed when we first met. Any restaurateur will tell you that one of the hardest spots to fill in the restaurant is the dish pit. Seeva has managed to inject humour and humanity into this otherwise dreary and difficult post. In addition, there has never been a time when I needed to worry about covering the position in his absence. Seeva always found someone to fill the gap.

JAMIE KENNEDY

Unlike the often stern, oppressive, hierarchical tone of many professional kitchens, there is a sense of joy and pleasure to the preparation of Jamie's food, which I believe is expressed on the plate. While precision and technique are important to Jamie, the people in his culinary family take precedence, and that family extends to all the farmers and artisans who supply his operations. Jamie takes pleasure in presenting the ingredients in a respectful, uncluttered manner, with a sense of modesty, rather than as an opportunity to impress with his personal technique. This generosity of spirit is also expressed in the progressive paid internships Jamie offered to a generation of hospitality professionals, who now spread this sense of joy and caring through operations across the country.

PAUL DECAMPO, FOOD ACTIVIST AND EDUCATOR

There are two things that Jamie Kennedy ingrained in me as a cook. The first is that good cooking is 50 percent skill and 50 percent knowing where your food is coming from and being connected with it. The second is that success in the kitchen is all about teamwork, and Chef J.K. always led by example. I saw him do everything from work the line to run food to load the dishwasher. If you were in the weeds, someone would always jump in and lend a hand and you'd always do the same for anyone. I also learned a lot of random classic rock trivia from Ken Steele.

JOSE ROSALES-LOPEZ, FORMER APPRENTICE, J.K. ALUMNI

In my many years of working with Jamie, I never saw him raise his voice, lose his temper or get upset. His grace, warmth and patience were the best lesson possible in this industry filled with hot tempers and bombast. He is the exact opposite of almost all the other chefs I have worked with, and this has completely influenced me in the way I work and the type of manager, chef and restaurateur I strive to be.

He is gutsy, and resilient, intelligent and very dignified. He is one of the kindest people I have ever known. He cooks with a purity and clarity that is completely unique— I feel I could recognize a Jamie dish without hesitation.

TOBEY NEMETH, FORMER HEAD CHEF AT J.K. WINE BAR,
CURRENTLY CHEF AND CO-OWNER OF EDULIS RESTAURANT, J.K. ALUMNI

I started with Jamie Kennedy Kitchens as a high-school co-op student. I was eighteen at the time. I honestly had no idea who Jamie Kennedy was before my co-op placement—my exposure to cooking and the rest of the culinary world was very limited at that point. I tried Googling him but all I got was info on the comedian of the same name.

One month after starting as a co-op student, I began to work weekends in the café. I had finally learned how highly regarded Jamie Kennedy was in the Canadian culinary scene. I then joined his apprenticeship program from 2008 until 2011, and I feel so fortunate to have done it all at JKK. Seriously, how many cooks under twenty years old can say that they've broken down half a pig?

CARLA MAYA, FORMER APPRENTICE, J.K. ALUMNI

Above: with pastry cook Mary Wood

Below: Thaya Mahesan

Below: Thayalan "Seeva" Thambithurai (*left*) and Julius Sunthar George

Above: with Ken Steele

I remember hearing about Ken Steele through a colleague who had worked with him. She said I should hire him, that he was really great. I called Ken to help with a big catering event I had landed at the Royal Ontario Museum. (This was a month before I opened my restaurant there.) The event was a huge success. Ken was awesome, and I remember approaching him while he was at the counter, getting every drop of mayonnaise from a mixing bowl with a spatula, thorough and meticulous. I offered him a job at my restaurant-to-be. He accepted. This was the beginning of a long working relationship that continues to this day. Like a married couple, over the years we began to understand each other on a profound level, completing each other's sentences and so on. Such is the way it is with us. In the kitchen we have a communication that requires few words. Rather, it requires an understanding of technique and style, and a commitment to excellence that is born of shared experience down through the years.

JAMIE KENNEDY

Jamie was my chef at the tail end of my apprenticeship. He was Canadian, he wasn't an asshole and he didn't mind black pepper on white things. His gentleness and generosity for those who really searched for the way was inspiring. He didn't just talk about the importance of the farmer thing. He exposed us to it. And back then the public didn't give a shit about that relationship, it wasn't the hip thing that it is now. Jamie did it for the right reasons and taught me that doing it for the right reasons will build a culture that ties front of house, back of house and purveyors together.

ANTHONY WALSH, EXECUTIVE CHEF, OLIVER & BONACINI RESTAURANTS

I met Thaya Mahesan at my restaurant in the museum. This was during the worst years of civil war in Sri Lanka. He had recently arrived from there with his young bride and was adjusting to his new life in Canada. I hired Thaya twenty years ago as a dishwasher. Today, like Ken, he is a pillar of our organization, sharing in the daily ritual that is so much a part of our brand: pursuing excellence in food production. Thaya has always cooked. He tells me stories of growing up in Sri Lanka and cooking for his family. He brings that same spirit of caring to his work with me.

JAMIE KENNEDY

My first day after I'd been hired as saucier, Jamie came up to me like we'd known each other forever. I had literally been there for three hours and he knew my name, he knew from my resumé that I'd been cooking in Portland and immediately started talking to me about Pinot Noir and how he had this farm and eventually wanted to start producing Pinot Noir from his farm. He made me feel so welcomed. It started on that day and it lasted for the entire three years that I worked for him.

SCOTT VIVIAN, CHEF AND CO-OWNER OF BEAST RESTAURANT, J.K. ALUMNI

BREAD

I've always been interested in baking, and baking bread at the restaurant is something I've done since the Palmerston days. I got turned on by the idea of sourdough and pain au levain. This is a traditional way to make bread from just three ingredients. Of course to do that you've got to start a culture with the wheat flour and water and feed it every day and nurture the starter meticulously to encourage a healthy yeast population. What happens then is that these yeasts start to populate your kitchen so that over time the bread takes on a life of its own. That whole idea of those three ingredients being able to produce leavened bread in the end was always appealing to me. I also believed in a holistic approach to restaurant production where I have minimized purchases of pre-made things. I have always believed in doing everything, that all the subsets of the trade of a cook should be observed somehow in the restaurant kitchen, and baking bread falls into that category. I believed in it also as a cost savings. I don't know if that's true or not at first, but once you reach a certain point of bread production where you fold it into the daily labour that you're already allocating in the kitchen, it might save you some dough. Ha ha.

Red Fife Sourdough Bread

Makes 2 loaves (about 1¼ pounds/625 g each)

As a kid I used to watch my aunt bake bread at her family cottage up north. I learned to mix commercial yeast into a dough. Then the dough would rise under a tea towel. I would watch while she punched the dough down and formed it into loaves to rise again before baking. I could hardly wait for the bread to be baked before I was there ready for a slice, the butter melting, the bread still warm from the oven.

This bread has one less ingredient, commercial yeast, but its success requires creating your own yeast. The process is simple but demands disciplined care and time.

Ingredients

Sourdough Starter

20 ounces (4¼ cups/550 g) organic unbleached hard white flour (used over 10 days)

2¼ cups (550 mL) water (used over 10 days)

Dough

19 ounces (4⅛ cups/520 g) organic unbleached hard white flour

4½ ounces (1 cup/125 g) Red Fife whole wheat flour

2 cups + 2 tablespoons (530 mL) water

6 ounces (170 g) sourdough starter

2½ teaspoons (14 g) salt

Directions

This recipe makes more starter than necessary for 2 loaves, but if you feed the starter (as described below) every few days to keep it alive (bubbling), you can bake fresh loaves regularly, as we do in the restaurant.

To make the sourdough starter, mix 3½ ounces (¾ cup/100 g) flour and 7 tablespoons (100 mL) water to form a stiff paste. Store in a clean vessel with a loose-fitting lid in a cool place. Each day, mix in 1¾ ounces (6 tablespoons/50 g) hard white flour and 3 tablespoons (50 mL) water. Your starter is ready when it is bubbling and emits a pleasant sour aroma. This should take about 10 days. Now you are ready to make bread. Store the starter in a cool place.

For the dough, combine the hard flour, Red Fife flour and water in a large bowl and mix until just combined, approximately 30 seconds. Place the sourdough starter and salt on top of the dough, on opposite sides from each other so they don't touch. Cover the bowl with plastic wrap and allow to sit for 15 minutes.

Using a stand mixer fitted with the dough hook, mix the dough on low speed for approximately 2 minutes. The dough will be quite wet, yet homogenous. Turn the dough into a large bowl, cover with plastic wrap and set aside in a warm place to ferment for approximately 2 hours and 45 minutes, punching the dough down once after 1 hour to expel air bubbles.

Punch the dough down again and turn it out onto a lightly floured surface. Cut the dough into 2 even pieces and shape each piece into a loose mass. Working with one mass of dough at a time (and keeping the other mass covered), knead with floured hands to form smooth, round loaves. Transfer the loaves to a floured baking sheet, placing them about 4 inches (10 cm) apart. Slide the baking sheet into a large plastic bag and allow loaves to rise at room temperature until roughly doubled in size, approximately 2 hours.

Meanwhile, preheat the oven to 400°F (200°C). Slash the tops of the loaves decoratively and bake until they are golden brown and sound hollow when tapped on the bottom, approximately 45 minutes. Cool on racks for approximately 1 hour before cutting.

A NOTE ON RED FIFE WHEAT

Red Fife is a heritage grain with a rich history in Canada. It used to be the predominant cultivar but was gradually pushed aside by varieties with a shorter growing season and higher yields and almost vanished altogether. I became aware of Red Fife wheat at the first Terra Madre—the international Slow Food symposium held in Italy—in 2004. There was a baker from the West Coast, Cliff Leir, who had learned about Red Fife from a grower in Saskatchewan. Cliff had a bakery in Victoria called Wild Fire and they were baking Red Fife sourdough breads in wood-fired ovens. He had brought his starter with him to Turin and he was making pain au levain with Red Fife dough at the Slow Food Presidia in the Salone del Gusto. There were kiosks there representing ingredients unique to their regions or countries and in danger of disappearing. Being at Terra Madre that year brought Red Fife the attention it needed to become commercially viable again.

Chicken Noodle Soup with Wild Rice Noodles

Makes 6 servings

There are some dishes that transcend fashion. There are some dishes that even transcend cultural diversity. Nobody, it seems, argues that chicken soup belongs solely to their tradition or their culture. Rather, chicken soup is exalted everywhere in the world as a nurturing elixir that cures the ills of the body and the soul. At the restaurant we serve the soup with pieces of chicken on the bone. I've simplified the recipe a little bit here.

I like to simmer a whole chicken in chicken stock for the version below. It is like a double dose of medicine. I add the wild rice twist to the standard noodle recipe to make it more like the true north strong and free.

Ingredients
Soup
1 chicken (4 pounds/2 kg)
12 cups (3 L) chicken stock
2 carrots, finely diced
2 celery stalks, finely diced
1 leek, halved lengthwise and thinly sliced
1 sprig of fresh thyme
12 black peppercorns
2 green onions, thinly sliced on the bias
2 tablespoons (30 mL) chopped fresh parsley

Wild Rice Pasta
4 eggs
1¼ cups (200 g) semolina
1½ cups (200 g) hard flour
⅔ cup (100 g) wild rice flour
1 teaspoon (5 mL) white wine vinegar
1 teaspoon (5 mL) olive oil
Salt

Directions
Place the chicken in a large stock pot. Add the chicken stock. Slowly bring to the boil over medium heat, then reduce heat and simmer for 2 hours, skimming from time to time. Remove chicken. When cool enough to handle, discard the skin and carefully pick all the meat from the bones, returning the bones to the stock pot. Reserve meat in the refrigerator. Continue to simmer the stock for 1 hour.

Meanwhile, make the wild rice pasta. In a large bowl, combine the eggs, semolina, hard flour, wild rice flour, vinegar, olive oil and salt to taste until the dough just comes together. Knead the dough on a lightly floured surface with the heel of your hand until the dough is smooth and workable but as dry as possible, about 10 minutes. Add a little water if needed to achieve the right consistency.

recipe continues . . .

313

Divide the dough into 6 pieces and roll each piece through a pasta machine until the second-narrowest setting is reached. Cut with a linguini cutter or with a knife to 7-inch (18 cm) lengths about ¼ inch (5 mm) wide. Spread noodles out on a baking sheet.

Strain the stock through a fine-mesh strainer. Discard the bones. Pour stock back into the pot and bring to the boil. Add all the chicken meat and return to the boil. Add the carrots, celery, leek, thyme and peppercorns. Simmer for 15 minutes. Add the noodles, cover and simmer for an additional 8 minutes. Remove thyme sprig.

Lay out 6 large bowls. Ladle soup into the bowls. Garnish with sliced green onions and chopped parsley. Serve.

314

Socca with Quick Ratatouille

Makes 4 servings

Socca is a type of pancake you would find if you were travelling in Nice, France. It originates there and is often sold on the streets, either plain or combined with other ingredients. Socca also has the additional charm of being gluten-free.

Ingredients

Socca
2 tablespoons (30 mL) fine olive oil
Pinch of salt
¾ cup plus 2 tablespoons (200 mL) water
1 cup (90 g) chickpea flour

Quick Ratatouille
¼ cup (60 mL) fine olive oil
1 medium onion, roughly chopped
2 cloves garlic, finely chopped
1 zucchini, cut into small pieces
1 red bell pepper, cut into small pieces
1 small eggplant, cut into small pieces
Salt and freshly ground black pepper
½ cup (125 mL) tomato sauce
1 ripe field tomato, seeded and diced
4 fresh basil leaves, thinly sliced

Directions

In a stainless steel bowl, combine the oil, salt and half the water. Add the chickpea flour. Whisk, adding water as required, to achieve a crêpe batter–like consistency (much like heavy cream). Allow the batter to rest at room temperature for 1 hour.

In a medium nonstick frying pan, make 4 crêpes with the socca batter (see page 52). These crêpes will be slightly thicker than regular crêpes. Place each crêpe on an ovenproof dinner plate.

To make the ratatouille, heat the olive oil in a large frying pan over medium heat. Add the onion, garlic, zucchini, red pepper, eggplant, and salt and pepper to taste. Simmer, stirring occasionally, for approximately 30 minutes or until the vegetables are tender.

Meanwhile, in a small saucepan, bring the tomato sauce to the boil. Add the diced tomato and the basil. Return to the boil, then add to the vegetable mixture. Bring the ratatouille back to the boil and simmer for 5 minutes.

Heat the plates with the socca in a 200°F (100°C) oven. Top the socca with the ratatouille. Serve.

Mussels Steamed in Riesling

Makes 4 servings

Riesling is a varietal that is produced more and more in Ontario as we discover how well the grape grows here. Riesling wines are crisp and fresh with a mineral backbone that speaks of the limestone found in the Niagara Escarpment. This dish was on the first menu when we launched Gilead Bistro in 2010.

316

Ingredients

2 tablespoons (30 mL) butter

2 cloves garlic, finely chopped

4 shallots, finely chopped

½ teaspoon (2 mL) chopped fresh thyme

48 mussels, scrubbed and debearded

1 cup (250 mL) Riesling

1 medium carrot, cut into julienne

1 small celery root, peeled and cut into julienne

2 tablespoons (30 mL) sun-dried tomatoes cut into julienne

2 tablespoons (30 mL) chopped fresh parsley

Directions

Melt the butter in a large saucepan. Add the garlic and shallots and gently sauté for 3 minutes. Add the thyme and mussels and sauté for an additional 1 minute. Add the Riesling, increase the heat and cover. Boil until mussels open, approximately 5 minutes. Discard any mussels that don't open.

Meanwhile, warm 4 large bowls. Arrange mussels in a pleasing pattern in each of the bowls. Distribute the julienned carrot, celery root and sun-dried tomatoes evenly on each arrangement of mussels. Pour cooking liquid over the vegetables and mussels. Sprinkle with the parsley. Serve immediately.

Pouding Chômeur

Makes 6 servings

This dessert came out of Quebec during the Depression. The name translates as "unemployment pudding" or "poor man's pudding." Maple syrup has such an addictive smoky and complex flavour. It is a luxury item, so it is difficult to believe that it would be associated with unemployment, but the recipe goes back to a time when the procurement of cane sugar would have been a special occasion and traditional maple syrup was a far more common source of sweetness.

Ingredients

¾ cup + 2 teaspoons (200 g) butter, softened

1 cup (250 mL) granulated sugar

2 eggs

3¼ cups (400 g) all-purpose flour

1 teaspoon (5 mL) baking powder

2 cups (500 mL) whipping cream

2 cups (500 mL) maple syrup

Directions

Cream the butter and sugar with an electric mixer until light and fluffy. Add the eggs, flour and baking powder and beat just until smooth. Do not over-mix. Refrigerate for at least 2 hours.

Preheat the oven to 400°F (200°C). Bring the cream and maple syrup to the boil in a saucepan, then reduce heat and simmer for 10 minutes.

Meanwhile, butter six 1-cup (250 mL) soufflé dishes. Divide the dough evenly among them. Place the dishes on a baking sheet. Pour the cream mixture evenly into the dishes. Bake for about 30 minutes or until a cake tester comes out clean. Serve.

319

Local Food Movement
Dinner—Soiled Reputation

Curried Sweet Potato and Swiss Chard Croquettes

Makes 6 servings

"Short eats" is the expression the *Ceylon Daily News Cookery Book* uses to describe what we call hors d'oeuvres. I think it is an apt name and also implies that there will be longer eats happening a little bit later. This recipe combines Tamil curry spicing with a North American tuber, the sweet potato. It is a wonderful short eat.

Ingredients

1 sweet potato

½ teaspoon (2 mL) cumin seeds

¼ teaspoon (1 mL) coriander seeds

1 green chili, very finely chopped

1 clove garlic, very finely chopped

½ teaspoon (2 mL) very finely chopped peeled fresh ginger

3 tablespoons (50 mL) yogurt

1 teaspoon (5 mL) roughly chopped fresh mint

1 cup (250 mL) sunflower oil

2 Swiss chard leaves, blanched, squeezed dry and roughly chopped

All-purpose flour for dredging

1 egg, beaten

1 cup (250 mL) dry breadcrumbs or panko

Directions

Preheat the oven to 350°F (180°C). Bake the sweet potato on a small baking sheet for approximately 1 hour or until it is soft and yielding to the touch.

Meanwhile, combine the cumin seeds and coriander seeds in a frying pan over medium heat. Toast the seeds, stirring regularly, until they are lightly toasted. Pulverize in a spice mill or coffee grinder. Mix the pulverized spices with the chili, garlic and ginger. Reserve.

Mix the yogurt with the chopped mint to make the raita. Reserve.

Heat the oil in a small saucepan to 350°F (180°C). Peel the sweet potato while it is still warm and transfer it to a small bowl. Mash it with a fork while incorporating the spice mixture and the Swiss chard. Form into balls the size of a large marble. Dredge the balls in the flour, coat in the beaten egg and then roll in the breadcrumbs, coating thoroughly.

Fry the croquettes in the oil, stirring continuously with a slotted spoon until they are crispy brown. Drain on paper towels. Place a small dollop of raita on each croquette. Serve.

Beef and Whitefish "Vitello Tonnato"

Makes 6 servings

Vitello tonnato is a classic cold dish from the Italian canon. Traditionally, it is made with thinly sliced roasted veal coated with a mayonnaise-based sauce mixed with minced cooked tuna with capers and anchovy. This adaptation uses beef, not veal, and whitefish instead of tuna, but the highly toned flavours of the classic remain.

Ingredients

Whitefish Mayonnaise

7 tablespoons (100 mL) fine olive oil
Sea salt
1 fresh skinless whitefish fillet (3½ ounces/100 g)
6 tablespoons (90 mL) cider mayonnaise
   (see recipe page 348)
6 anchovy fillets, finely chopped
2 tablespoons (30 mL) capers, finely chopped
2 tablespoons (30 mL) finely chopped fresh chives
Juice of ½ lemon
Freshly ground black pepper

Beef

⅔ pound (350 g) beef tenderloin steak
Sea salt and freshly ground black pepper
¼ cup (60 mL) sunflower oil
2 cups (500 mL) Pinot Noir wine
Freshly grated horseradish
¼ cup (60 mL) fine olive oil

Directions

To make the whitefish mayonnaise, warm the oil in a saucepan to 150°F (65°C). Lightly salt the whitefish fillet and place in the warmed oil. Cook for about 10 minutes or until the flesh turns opaque. Remove from the oil and let cool.

In a bowl, mix the cider mayonnaise with the anchovies, capers, chives, lemon juice, and salt and pepper to taste. Flake the cooked whitefish into the mayonnaise mixture. Mix well and reserve, refrigerated.

For the beef, preheat the oven to 325°F (160°C).

Season the steak with salt and pepper. Heat the sunflower oil in an ovenproof frying pan over medium-high heat until it is almost smoking. Sear the steak on both sides, then transfer the pan to the oven. Roast steak for 5 minutes. Transfer steak to a plate and cool to room temperature, then refrigerate until cold, at least 2 hours and preferably overnight.

Thinly slice the cold beef. Spread a thin layer of the mayonnaise mixture on the bottom of a shallow rectangular pan. Top with a layer of beef. Repeat layering until all the mayonnaise and all the beef is used up, ending with a layer of beef.

In a medium saucepan, bring the Pinot Noir to a boil and then reduce the heat to let it gently simmer until it has significantly reduced in volume and is syrupy.

Set out 6 salad plates. Cut the vitello tonnato into 6 pieces. Spoon some Pinot Noir glaze onto each plate, place a portion of the vitello tonnato into the centre of the plate and finish with a grating of fresh horseradish and a drizzle of olive oil.

Ginger Cake Trifle with Preserved Summer Fruits

Makes 8 to 10 servings

In the summertime, we take advantage of the bounty of local fruits and preserve them in simple syrup. This recipe celebrates that bounty in an adaptation of a classic English dessert.

Ingredients

Crème Anglaise

4 cups (1 L) whole milk

1 cup (200 g) granulated sugar

10 egg yolks

¼ cup (60 mL) cold whipping cream

1 vanilla bean, split lengthwise and seeds
    scooped out

1 capful vanilla extract

Ginger Cake

½ cup (125 g) butter, softened

½ cup (110 g) brown sugar

2 eggs

1 cup (250 mL) molasses

½ cup (125 mL) brewed coffee, cooled

½ cup (125 mL) water

2½ cups (300 g) all-purpose flour

2 teaspoons (10 mL) baking soda

1 tablespoon (15 mL) ground ginger

2 teaspoons (10 mL) ground cinnamon

1 teaspoon (5 mL) ground allspice

½ teaspoon (2 mL) freshly grated nutmeg

½ teaspoon (2 mL) salt

¼ teaspoon (1 mL) ground cloves

Assembly

1 cup (250 mL) whipping cream

3 tablespoons (50 mL) kirsch

3 cups (750 mL) Preserved Summer Fruits in
    Syrup (see recipe page 286), drained and sliced

Directions

To make the crème anglaise, combine the milk and sugar in a saucepan and scald. Remove from the heat and whisk in the egg yolks all at once. Return to low heat and stir constantly with a wooden spoon until thickened enough to coat the back of the spoon (about the consistency of house paint). Strain into a bowl. Stir in the cream, vanilla seeds and vanilla extract. Place plastic wrap directly on the surface and store in the refrigerator for up to 1 week.

To make the ginger cake, preheat the oven to 325°F (160°C). Grease and flour a 9-inch (1.5 L) round cake pan.

Cream the butter and brown sugar with an electric mixer until light and fluffy. Add the eggs, molasses, coffee and water and beat just until combined. Sift together the flour, baking soda, ginger, cinnamon, allspice, nutmeg, salt and cloves. Add to the wet mixture, mixing just until

recipe continues . . .

combined. Pour batter into the prepared pan and bake until a wooden skewer comes out clean, approximately 45 minutes. Cool in pan for 30 minutes before turning out the cake and slicing horizontally into 4 thin layers.

To assemble the trifle, whip the cream into stiff peaks. Fold in the crème anglaise. Place a thin layer of cake in the bottom of a large glass bowl. Sprinkle with a little of the kirsch. Spread one-quarter of the preserved fruits over the cake. Cover with one-third of the cream mixture. Repeat layering until the bowl is full, ending with a layer of fruit. Chill for 2 hours before serving. If preferred, this dish may also be layered in individual serving dishes, but start and end with cream mixture, as pictured.

Roots

In Ontario, we rely on root vegetables as a staple through the cold winter months. They contribute their earthy warmth to some of the best comfort foods in our repertoire.

In those years when, by Christmas, the ground is still not frozen solid, I go out to my garden and dig up sunchokes, parsnips and leeks. Guests at the table always notice the special sweetness these vegetables bring. Often in creating dishes using this post-summer bounty, I include some vestige of the summer in the form of a garnish such as semi-cured tomatoes (see recipe page 137) or a winter-grown greenhouse green like arugula or radish seedling.

331

Raw Winter Vegetable Salad with Vegetable Juices

Makes 6 servings

Winter in Southern Ontario can be dreary and grey. When we approach food production and menu planning in the local context, sometimes we need to use our imaginations to bring vivid colour to the dull palette of winter. This salad uses mainly storage vegetables with a scattering of greenhouse greens to let the sun in.

Ingredients

4 orange carrots, scrubbed
4 deep purple carrots, scrubbed
2 yellow carrots, scrubbed
2 valentine radishes, thinly sliced
2 candy-cane beets, scrubbed and thinly sliced
1 small yellow beet, scrubbed and thinly sliced
1 small red beet, scrubbed and thinly sliced
2 shallots, finely chopped
¼ cup (60 mL) cider vinegar
Salt and freshly ground black pepper
2 tablespoons (30 mL) sunflower seedlings
2 tablespoons (30 mL) arugula seedlings
¼ cup (60 mL) fine olive oil

Directions

Using a centrifugal juicer, juice separately 2 orange carrots and 2 deep purple carrots, reserving the juices separately. Using a mandoline, very thinly slice the remaining carrots, the radishes and the beets. Transfer them to a bowl of ice water. In a small bowl, drench the shallots with the cider vinegar.

Lay out 6 salad plates. Pour a pool of each colour of carrot juice on each plate. Drain all the vegetable slices and dry them in a salad spinner. Place the slices in a large bowl. Drain the shallots and toss with the vegetables. Season with salt and pepper. Stacking the vegetables in your hand, form 2 stacks of alternating vegetable slices for each plate and place them on the pool of carrot juices.

Garnish each plate with a sprinkling of sunflower and arugula seedlings. Drizzle with the olive oil and serve.

Flageolets with Carrots and Soubise

Makes 4 servings

Flageolets are a variety of dried bean that typically accompany lamb in the French canon. In this recipe I wanted to highlight their beautiful pale green colour against a palette of white and orange.

Ingredients

8 ounces (250 g) fresh flageolet beans (or 6 ounces/ 180 g dried, soaked in water overnight, then drained)

1 clove garlic, thinly sliced

12 pearl onions, peeled

4 carrots (various heirloom varieties), scrubbed and thickly sliced on the bias

1 bay leaf

1 sprig of fresh thyme

Salt

4 medium onions, thinly sliced

¾ cup (190 g) butter

Cider vinegar

Directions

Place beans, garlic, pearl onions, carrots, bay leaf and thyme in a large saucepan. Cover with cold water and bring to the boil. Reduce heat and simmer until beans are very tender, approximately 30 minutes. Season with salt, and discard the bay leaf.

Meanwhile, to make the soubise, place sliced onions and butter in a saucepan and cook slowly until onions are transparent but not browned, approximately 30 minutes. Transfer to a blender and blend until smooth. Season with salt and a touch of cider vinegar.

Warm an oval baking dish in the oven. Pour the soubise over the base of the dish. With a slotted spoon, place the bean and carrot mixture on top. Serve immediately.

Endives with Fried Garlic

Makes 6 servings

There's something about crisp, bitter endive and radicchio served with a warm dressing that's so adult. This is a salad for grown-ups. You can really only make this kind of salad using winter lettuces because they are hardy enough to take the heat without wilting.

Ingredients

Croutons

6 slices white bread, crusts removed

3 tablespoons (50 mL) rendered duck fat

18 lardons (thick rectangles about 2 inches/
  5 cm long) of smoked side bacon

Fried Garlic

¼ cup (60 mL) olive oil

2 cloves garlic, thinly sliced

Salad

1 Belgian endive, torn into small pieces

1 head frisée (curly endive), torn into small pieces

1 head radicchio, torn into small pieces

12 pieces semi-cured tomatoes (see recipe page 137)

Dressing

3 tablespoons (50 mL) sunflower oil

1 shallot, finely chopped

1 clove garlic, finely chopped

1 tablespoon (15 mL) cider vinegar

Salt and freshly ground black pepper

Directions

To make the croutons, preheat the oven to 275°F (140°C). Place the bread, duck fat and bacon lardons on a baking sheet. Place in the oven and slowly toast the bread slices, turning once, until they are golden on both sides; remove from oven. Remove the lardons when they are crisp and transfer them to paper towels to drain.

Meanwhile, make the fried garlic. In a small frying pan, heat the olive oil over low heat. Add the garlic slices and slowly fry them, stirring regularly, until they are golden brown. Drain garlic on paper towels and wipe out the pan.

To assemble the salad, place the Belgian endive, frisée, radicchio and semi-cured tomatoes in a bowl. Reserve.

For the dressing, heat the sunflower oil in the frying pan over medium heat. Add the shallot and garlic and sauté until the garlic starts to change colour. Add the vinegar and remove from the heat. Season with salt and pepper.

Place a crouton on each plate. Pour the hot dressing over the lettuces and toss. Place an equal amount of salad on each of the croutons. Sprinkle with the crisp lardons and fried garlic. Serve at once.

Borscht with Crème Fraîche and Goulash Paste

Makes 6 servings

One winter when I was much younger, I worked at the Derby Hotel in the village of Davos, Switzerland. The local cuisine was inspired by many European traditions, and from Austria and the Austro-Hungarian Empire came dishes like goulash. In particular, a mixture of herbs and spices caught my attention, as it was used to boost the flavour of the goulash at the point of serving. Here I have adapted that mixture to a soup whose origins are also in eastern Europe—beet borscht.

Beets grow very well here in Southern Ontario and are readily available in a rainbow of colours and myriad shapes. This soup uses traditional red beets that are cooked first with a little vinegar, which helps to fix the deep red colour that is so appealing in the finished soup.

Ingredients

6 medium red beets
3 tablespoons (50 mL) white wine vinegar
¼ cup (60 mL) sunflower oil
2 medium onions, thinly sliced
½ small green cabbage, thinly sliced
2 medium Yukon Gold potatoes, peeled and
 thinly sliced
12 cups (3 L) vegetable stock
Salt and freshly ground black pepper
2 tablespoons (30 mL) chopped fresh dill
2 tablespoons (30 mL) chopped fresh parsley
1 teaspoon (5 mL) chopped lemon peel
1 teaspoon (5 mL) finely chopped garlic
1 teaspoon (5 mL) caraway seeds, finely chopped
 (chop the caraway seeds with some chopped
 parsley or dill to prevent them from jumping
 all over the cutting board)
6 tablespoons (90 mL) crème fraîche or yogurt

Directions

Place the beets in a large saucepan. Cover with water and add the vinegar. Simmer until tender, approximately 1 hour. Drain the beets and let cool slightly. When they are cool enough to handle, slip off the skins and slice the beets into pieces any size and shape you like.

Meanwhile, in a large soup pot, heat the oil over medium heat. Add the onions, cabbage and potatoes and gently sauté for approximately 15 minutes, stirring from time to time. Add the vegetable stock and bring to the boil. Reduce heat to a simmer and cook for about 15 minutes. Add the sliced beets and continue cooking for an additional 10 minutes. Season with salt and pepper.

Meanwhile, to make the goulash paste, combine the dill, parsley, lemon peel, garlic and caraway seeds.

Lay out 6 bowls. Ladle soup into each bowl. Place a dollop of crème fraîche in the centre of each bowl. Sprinkle a liberal amount of goulash paste on each dollop. Serve.

Lentils and Quinoa on Grilled Sweet Potato

Makes 4 servings

I remember years ago hanging out with Rastafarians in the hills of St. Lucia. Rastafarians are strict vegetarians and they divided the vegetable kingdom roughly into two categories: "food" and "ital." "Food" comprised heavy, starchy roots and legumes like dasheen and pigeon peas, and "ital" covered off everything else, such as fruits and vegetables that grow above ground. "What about nuts?" I asked. "Nuts are nuts, mon—just eat them."

This dish falls on the "food" side of things.

Ingredients

1 small buttercup squash
2 tablespoons (30 mL) butter
1 tablespoon (15 mL) finely chopped peeled fresh
    ginger
1 clove garlic, finely chopped
A good pinch of freshly grated nutmeg
Salt and freshly ground black pepper
2 sweet potatoes
1 tablespoon (15 mL) cider vinegar
½ cup (125 mL) green lentils
½ cup (125 mL) quinoa (any colour), well rinsed
3 cups (750 mL) water
2 shallots, thinly sliced
¼ cup (60 mL) white wine vinegar
2 tablespoons (30 mL) chopped fresh parsley
¼ cup (60 mL) fine olive oil

Directions

Preheat the oven to 325°F (160°C). Cut the squash in half and pull out and discard all the seeds. Place the squash cut side up on a baking sheet. Place half of the butter in each cavity and season with the ginger, garlic, nutmeg, and salt and pepper to taste. Place the sweet potatoes on the baking sheet. Bake for about 1 hour or until the potatoes and squash flesh yield to the touch.

When the squash is cool enough to handle, scrape the flesh into a blender. Add the cider vinegar and blend with enough water to bring the purée to sauce consistency. Peel the sweet potatoes and cut into thick slices. Reserve.

Meanwhile, simmer the lentils and quinoa in the water for 15 to 20 minutes or until just tender. Drain.

In a medium bowl, mix the shallot slices and white wine vinegar. Add the cooked quinoa and lentils and the chopped parsley. Season with salt and pepper and toss well.

Grill the slices of sweet potato for about 5 minutes on both sides, being careful not to burn them.

Lay out 4 plates. Arrange the slices of sweet potato in an overlapping pattern on the plates. Spoon some of the quinoa-lentil mixture into the centre of each plate. Drizzle with the olive oil. Pour the squash sauce all around the sweet potatoes. Serve.

Parsnip and Apple Mash

Makes 8 servings

Try this interesting combination with your turkey at Thanksgiving dinner or with roasted pork. It makes a lovely sweet and savoury accompaniment.

Ingredients

10 ounces (300 g) peeled and roughly
    chopped parsnips
½ cup (125 mL) sweet apple cider
¾ cup (190 g) butter
10 ounces (300 g) peeled, cored and chopped crisp
    sweet-tart apples such as Cortland
Salt and freshly ground black pepper

Directions

Preheat the oven to 350°F (180°C). Place the parsnips, cider and half of the butter in a baking dish. Cover with foil and bake for 1 hour or until parsnips are tender. Add the apples, cover and bake for an additional 15 minutes.

Mash the parsnips and apples, adding the remaining butter gradually as you mash. Season with salt and pepper. Serve.

Roast and Confit of Duck with Roasted Potatoes and Sour Cherries

Makes 4 servings

It is interesting how, when people describe the taste of wine, most of the time they say that the taste reminds them of some flavour or aroma of fruit other than grapes. As in, "This Pinot Noir tastes like cherries." When I walked into my barn one day, the aroma of fermenting Pinot Noir grapes from the year's harvest filled the space like a thick fog. At this early stage, the smell was of grapes, a kind of stewed, heavy, rich grapey aroma. It was warm and inviting. Later the wine would take on accents of strawberries and cherries. This recipe is meant to go with Pinot Noir and will strike a cherry chord.

Several varieties of duck are on the market today. The one I like the most is Muscovy, because they are so meaty, but Pekin and Moulard are also very good. If you are fortunate enough to have access to wild ducks, they offer the best flavour of all.

Ingredients

1 fresh duck (about 4 pounds/2 kg)

A generous sprinkling of coarse salt

2 cloves garlic, thinly sliced

2 bay leaves

12 black peppercorns, cracked

2 cups (500 mL) + 2 tablespoons (30 mL) rendered duck or chicken fat

Salt and freshly ground black pepper

½ cup (125 mL) white wine

12 sour cherries, pitted

4 teaspoons (20 mL) granulated sugar

8 new potatoes

1 leek, cut into thin strips

Directions

Remove the legs from the duck. Place the legs in a baking dish. Sprinkle with the coarse salt, garlic, bay leaves and peppercorns. Cover and place in the refrigerator for 2 hours.

Preheat the oven to 250°F (120°C).

In a saucepan, melt 2 cups (500 mL) duck fat over medium heat. Pour over the salted duck legs. Bake for 4 hours or until the thigh bone comes away from the leg easily. Cool in the fat, then cover and refrigerate overnight.

Preheat the oven to 400°F (200°C). Remove the 2 breasts from the duck. Season with salt. Place the breasts skin-side down in a large cast-iron frying pan over medium-low heat. Gently sauté the breasts, without moving them, for about 10 minutes or until the skin is deep golden brown. Flip the breasts over and sear for about 1 minute. Flip them onto the skin side again, transfer, in the pan, to the oven and roast for about 8 minutes. The flesh should still be quite rare. Transfer breasts to a cutting board.

Pour off the fat and deglaze the pan with the white wine. Boil the wine until it has reduced by half. Add the sour cherries and sugar and simmer for 10 minutes.

Meanwhile, remove the confit legs from their fat. Cut the legs in half at the joint and place on a small baking sheet. Roast for about 20 minutes or until bubbling and golden brown.

While the duck legs are crisping, cook the potatoes in boiling salted water just until tender. Drain. When cool enough to handle, cut them in half. Slowly fry them in 2 tablespoons (30 mL) duck fat. When they are golden brown on all sides, add the strips of leek. Gently sauté for 5 minutes or until the leeks soften. Remove from the heat and season with salt and pepper.

Lay out 4 dinner plates. Place a small pile of the potato and leek mixture on each plate. Arrange a piece of duck confit on each plate. Spoon a pool of sour cherry compote around the duck. Finally, carve each duck breast into 8 slices. Place 4 slices on each plate in a fan pattern against the piece of duck confit. Serve.

French Fries and Philosophy

French fries, for me, started as a political statement. I didn't want to be known as a fancy chef, but I was at odds with the limited access the public had to my kind of cooking. Very few people could afford to pay for dinner in my restaurant given the way that I'd been taught how to cook, and that troubled me. I also observed and tasted what the mass market had to offer in the fast-food sector and was alarmed at the low bar we seemed to have set for ourselves. Early on I had a desire to appeal to a broader audience. My idea was that well-crafted food could go head to head with industrial food at the same price point. When I looked at what was being served in chain restaurants and food courts, at ball games and hockey rinks, on airplanes and at bus stations, in school cafeterias and even in hospitals, it was all at a very low bar. This was before any kind of backlash against fast food. It bothered me that good cooking outside the home was only available to the elite of society, and at the other end the quality was, generally speaking, much lower.

Back in the early '80s, when I was in Paris, I had a girlfriend who worked at the Eiffel Tower selling souvenirs and I would go and wait for her at the base of the tower. There was a woman who would roll up in a small van and sell french fries. She had her own little painted sign and she sold french fries and sorbet. This was Paris, after all. I ordered fries from her a lot because they were so delicious. She very carefully selected the potatoes as well as the oil for frying and the mayonnaise that she served with them. All of those things made the experience so much better than I had anticipated when I first ordered the fries from her. I thought, okay, this is something I can do back in North America. Just to raise the bar a little.

I started out using peanut oil because it was the best tasting. The potatoes I had in France were a yellow-fleshed Dutch varietal that was kind of waxy, and the closest I could find to them in Canada were Yukon Golds. I used two types of salt. I stopped using peanut oil because of allergies, and I tried canola, but the flavour is way too bold for fries, too full of character, plus most canola is genetically modified now. I settled on sunflower oil, which has a nice mild flavour that is perfect for fries. My french fries bridged the elitism of fine dining with the mass market of fast food. Today, even though people are more sophisticated in their diets, french fries are not going away.

French Fries

Makes 4 servings

I've been using french fries to tell a local story for a long time. A few years ago I switched from using lemons to local cider vinegar in the mayonnaise. More recently, my cousin Colin and his son Jeff connected with a farmer in Cobourg, Ontario, to grow sunflowers and produce oil for their fry stand operation on the same farm. Now I have access to this beautiful local sunflower oil for my fries.

Ingredients

6 medium Yukon Gold potatoes
10 cups (2.5 L) sunflower oil
1 tablespoon (15 mL) roughly chopped
    fresh thyme
Fine and coarse salt

Directions

Peel the potatoes and cut them into evenly sized sticks of whatever thickness you prefer.

In a large, deep, heavy pot, heat the oil to 250°F (120°C). Blanch the potatoes in the oil until they appear to be somewhat cooked but are not yet turning golden. Remove them with a slotted spoon or skimmer and spread them out on a baking sheet to cool.

Heat the oil to 350°F (180°C). Fry the potatoes until they are golden brown, within a few minutes. Keep an eye on them—they'll brown up gradually. Transfer them to a large bowl. Toss the fries with the thyme and salts. Serve at once with mayonnaise.

My brother Jack and I started coming down to the Brick Works before they had a market— my dad was helping with the planning for that. My dad and I decided that we'd do fries there every week, and since then it's been going really well. It's such a simple thing, just like so many of his dishes, something you elevate by just taking the proper steps, using the best ingredients, and you end up with these amazing results.

MICHA KENNEDY, SON

Cider Mayonnaise

Makes 2 cups (500 mL)

Ontario has so many apple orchards, but today, more farms are growing fewer cultivars. If you hunt a little, you will still discover apple farmers who are growing a variety of heirloom apples. It was challenging to find a good substitute for lemon juice in the mayonnaise, but eventually I found Filsinger's organic cider vinegar. It has an excellent flavour and gentle acidity.

Ingredients

3 egg yolks, at room temperature
¼ cup (60 mL) Filsinger's cider vinegar
¼ cup (60 mL) Kozlik's Daily Dijon mustard, at room temperature
2 cups (500 mL) sunflower oil
Salt

Directions

In a medium stainless steel bowl, combine the egg yolks, cider vinegar and mustard. Whisk until smooth. While still whisking, add the oil in a slow, steady stream. When the oil has been emulsified into the other ingredients, the mayonnaise should be fairly stiff. Season with salt.

Transfer to a lidded jar and store in the fridge for up to 2 weeks.

Chili Mayonnaise

Makes 2 cups (500 mL)

When we started bringing our fries to the Air Canada Centre for the Leafs and Raptors games, we developed a new mayonnaise made with serrano chilies. It was a big hit, especially during hockey games between the Leafs and their arch rivals, Les Habitants.

Ingredients

2 red serrano chilies

Generous ⅓ cup (75 mL) drained roasted red peppers (see recipe page 293), at room temperature

3 egg yolks, at room temperature

¼ cup (60 mL) cider vinegar

¼ cup (60 mL) Dijon mustard, at room temperature

2 cups (500 mL) sunflower oil

Salt

Directions

In a blender, combine the chilies, roasted red peppers, egg yolks, vinegar and mustard. Blend on high speed. Reduce speed to slow and add the sunflower oil in a slow, steady stream. When the oil has been emulsified into the other ingredients, the mayonnaise should be fairly stiff. Season with salt.

Transfer to a lidded jar and store in the fridge for up to 2 weeks.

Poutine with Braised Beef and Aged Cheddar

Makes 6 servings

I love poutine. I think the concept of the dish is genius, and it's such a delicious savoury hit to the body and mind. It is one of those dishes that I have focused on over the years. I like to apply my own sensibilities to the standard version that I imagine hungry truck drivers, eager to put miles behind them, wolf down at *routiers* in Quebec.

This recipe won a magazine poutine taste challenge in Toronto in 2012. My favourite Southern Ontario cheddars are Wilton and Black River.

Ingredients

Braised Beef in Gravy

¼ cup (60 mL) all-purpose flour

½ cup (125 mL) lard

2 pounds (1 kg) stewing beef (chuck, shank or flank)

2 pounds (1 kg) mirepoix (equal amounts of roughly chopped onion, carrot and celery, and 3 cloves garlic, thickly sliced)

3 tablespoons (50 mL) crushed canned tomatoes

8 cups (2 L) beef stock

3 bay leaves

12 black peppercorns, coarsely ground

2 tablespoons (30 mL) fresh thyme leaves, chopped

Poutine

French fries (see recipe page 347), made with 9 medium Yukon Gold potatoes

6 ounces (180 g) 2-year-old local cheddar, grated

4 cups (1 L) braised beef in gravy

3 green onions, thinly sliced on the bias

6 tablespoons (90 mL) sour cream

Directions

To make the braised beef, bake the flour on a baking sheet in a 400°F (200°C) oven, stirring from time to time, until nicely browned, approximately 1 hour.

recipe continues . . .

(Roasting the flour makes for a more richly flavoured roux. You may like to bake a cup of flour and reserve the remainder in a jar for future use.) Leave the oven on.

In a roasting pan, heat ¼ cup (60 mL) of the lard on the stove over medium heat. Sear the beef in the hot fat on all sides; remove to a plate and reserve. Stir the mirepoix into the roasting pan and roast in the oven until the vegetables are evenly browned, about 30 minutes. Add the tomatoes and continue roasting until the liquid has all evaporated and the colour is deepening. Reduce oven temperature to 275°F (140°C).

Place the roasting pan on the stove over medium heat and add the beef stock. Bring to the boil. Add the bay leaves, peppercorns and thyme. Reduce heat to a simmer and add the beef and any accumulated juices. Cover, return to the oven and braise until beef is very tender, approximately 1½ hours.

Strain braising liquid from the meat, reserving the liquid. Discard the mirepoix. Shred meat and reserve.

In a saucepan over medium heat, melt the remaining ¼ cup (60 mL) lard. Add 2 tablespoons (30 mL) browned flour and stir for 3 minutes. Gradually add the braising liquid, stirring continuously until you have a thin gravy consistency. Cook, stirring from time to time, for 1 hour.

Add shredded beef to the gravy and bring to the boil. Reduce heat and gently simmer for 10 minutes.

While the beef simmers, make the french fries. After tossing the fries with thyme and both salts, add the grated cheese and toss well.

Set out 6 warmed cereal bowls. Divide the fries evenly among them. Ladle the hot braised beef into each bowl. Sprinkle with sliced green onions and drizzle with sour cream. Serve immediately.

Opposite: with Flavia "Flavour-Flav" Poon

family life

LIKE THE DIFFERENT STAGES OF

CHILDHOOD MY FAMILY IS CONSTANTLY EVOLVING.

AS WE GROW OLDER IT IS SO GRATIFYING FOR ME

TO SEE THEIR APPRECIATION FOR THE

IMPORTANCE OF TAKING TIME TOGETHER

TO BE AROUND THE TABLE.

Cooking for the Kids

I have four children: Julia, Micha, Jackson and Nile. We often made spaghetti Bolognese for supper. I'd bring home the meat and then I'd help Nile set up the little grinder and he would grind the meat, hand-cranking it. My kids saw how much attention I was paying to the ingredients and the length of time things take to cook, and this made them understand that cooking was a process and that you had to have respect for the process. We made pizza from scratch, and we'd cook the pizza on a stone. We did stir-fries with rice; steaks crusted with garlic, thyme, pepper and paprika; pasta with olives and rosemary. Olives! Julia was so picky, she'd never eat olives and then suddenly, just like magic, she became accepting of many different foods that she'd spurned in the past. Now all of them have developed a broad palate and respect for the process of making good food.

Something as simple as scrambled eggs the *special-trick* way (slowly and methodically) really taught them how to approach gastronomy with respect. For instance, they know how to carry themselves in restaurants, they know how to use the cutlery, they engage the server each time they come to the table, make room for them to set something down, look them in the eye and thank them. It's great. I'm really proud of my kids the way they are around the culture.

The way he cooks a steak is so simple. It's just chopped garlic, salt and pepper, whatever herbs are on hand, maybe lovage or parsley, crust the steak with that and sear it. That was one of my favourites growing up and now when I make steak I do it that way.

NILE KENNEDY, SON

Once when I was little I went to Bear Lake with my dad to visit our cousins. I wore nothing but underwear and a lifejacket for three days, and when my mum arrived my face was smeared with berry juice and my hair was dreaded with leaves and twigs.

We saw farmers and visited restaurants. I grew up with Michael Stadtländer and his sons of similar age. It was us who would run naked through the woods with lips greasy from the pig skin ripping between our teeth. For my sixteenth birthday I was presented with a 1984 bottle of La Tâche Burgundy.

JULIA KENNEDY, DAUGHTER

I'm perfectly happy when I'm at the farm, just barbecuing with my dad. Burgers or steaks, some grilled veggies, we keep it pretty simple out at the farm. I love going to the beach at Sandbanks. Any chance to spend time in that part of Ontario, I'll take it.

JACKSON KENNEDY, SON

Egg Nog

Makes 12 servings

This recipe defines decadence and is a must-have over the holiday season. I can only describe it as a pillowy, frothy cloud with a kick. Of course, we serve a rum-free version to the kids.

Ingredients

12 eggs, separated
1½ cups (375 mL) amber rum
1¼ cups (150 g) icing sugar
4 cups (1 L) whipping cream
Freshly ground nutmeg

Directions

In a stainless steel bowl, whisk together the egg yolks, rum and icing sugar. Refrigerate, covered, overnight.

The next day, whisk the egg whites in a very clean stainless steel bowl until soft peaks form. Stir the whipping cream into the egg yolk mixture. Fold in the egg whites. Pour into a decorative bowl and grate nutmeg over the entire surface. Ladle into cups and enjoy!

Cheesy Scrambled Eggs on Toasted Red Fife Bread

Makes 6 servings

Throughout their childhood my children and I didn't get to spend a lot of time together. The restaurants and catering certainly took up much of my time. Sundays usually worked out, though, as a family day. One of the Sunday rituals was to have these scrambled eggs for breakfast. We had a lovely chive patch in the garden. One of the children was always dispatched to harvest the necessary chives to finish the dish.

Ingredients

1 cup (250 g) butter

1 large onion, finely diced

12 eggs

1¼ cups (75 g) finely grated Parmigiano-Reggiano

3 tablespoons (50 mL) milk

6 slices Red Fife sourdough bread (see recipe page 310), toasted and buttered

2 tablespoons (30 mL) finely chopped fresh chives

Directions

In a large shallow saucepan, melt the butter over low heat. Add the onion and cook, stirring regularly, for 30 minutes or until translucent but not browned.

Whisk the eggs and add to the onion. Cook, stirring continuously, until the eggs begin to coagulate. Once the eggs appear to be drying, stir in the grated cheese, then the milk. Remove from the heat.

Arrange the buttered toast on 6 plates. Share the eggs evenly on each piece of toast. Sprinkle with chopped chives. Serve.

We enjoy his slow scrambled eggs on Sunday mornings with hot buttered J.K. sourdough and it is delicious. Our family drinks pots of excellent French-pressed coffee and my dad leans back with his hands stretched over his head. He takes the most toast of all. His favourite thing is toast.

JULIA KENNEDY, DAUGHTER

Steel-Cut Oats Porridge with Steamed Milk and Maple Syrup

Makes 4 servings

Every two years, I participate in a wonderful event called Porridge for Parkinson's. It is a breakfast event aimed at raising funds for and awareness of the battle against Parkinson's disease.

I have always preferred the taste and texture of steel-cut oats versus rolled oats. This is how I serve them at the event with the offer of a drizzle of Scotch whisky to top it all off.

Ingredients

¾ cup (175 mL) steel-cut oats

2 cups (500 mL) cold water

Pinch of salt

2 cups (500 mL) milk

Maple syrup for drizzling

4 teaspoons (20 mL) Scotch whisky

Directions

Mix the oats, water and salt in a large saucepan and place over medium heat. Cook, stirring regularly, for approximately 30 minutes or until the mixture has thickened.

Steam (or heat and whisk) the milk. Divide the porridge among 4 bowls. Pour steamed milk on top and drizzle with maple syrup. Sprinkle each bowl with 1 teaspoon (5 mL) of your favourite Scotch whisky. Serve.

Chicken Liver Pâté

Makes 4 half-pint (250 mL) jars

This recipe began as a Kennedy family classic. My mum read about a French chef who worked at the White House during the Kennedy administration, and she adapted certain recipes from the Christmas holidays at the White House for our own Kennedy family Christmas. The recipe for the chicken liver pâté has evolved over the years but is still found on my table at Christmastime and is always on the menu at Gilead. According to Ivy Knight, it is the best chicken liver pâté on earth.

Ingredients

1⅔ cups (400 g) + 6 tablespoons (100 g) butter

3 onions, thinly sliced

3 cloves garlic, finely minced

3 apples (any kind), peeled, cored and roughly diced

1 teaspoon (5 mL) ground fenugreek

1 teaspoon (5 mL) turmeric

1¼ pounds (625 g) fresh chicken livers

2 tablespoons (30 mL) brandy

2 tablespoons (30 mL) dry sherry

1 tablespoon (15 mL) chopped fresh parsley

1 teaspoon (5 mL) chopped fresh thyme

Salt and freshly ground black pepper

Directions

In a large pot over medium-low heat, melt 1⅔ cups (400 g) butter. Add the onions, garlic, apples, fenugreek and turmeric. Gently cook, stirring from time to time, for approximately 2 hours. It is important to thoroughly cook the onions but without browning them at all.

Meanwhile, melt 6 tablespoons (100 g) butter in a large frying pan over high heat. Quickly sauté the chicken livers, being careful not to overcook them. They should remain soft to the touch. Add the brandy and set it alight. When the flames have died down, stir in the sherry, parsley and thyme. Remove from the heat.

Transfer the liver mixture to a blender. Add the apple mixture. Blend at high speed until smooth. Season with salt and pepper. Pour the pâté into 4 half-pint (250 mL) mason jars. Seal and refrigerate. Serve with pickles and crusty bread.

Pâté keeps, refrigerated, for up to 1 week.

Duck Chawanmushi

Makes 4 servings

When the kids were small it was challenging to find restaurants to take them to where we could have some semblance of a dining experience amid the unrelenting challenge of keeping them happy. Masa Japanese restaurant was a perennial favourite because they had these tables for six that were completely enclosed, and it was customary to remove your shoes. The kids loved that, and I loved that they couldn't escape and disturb the other patrons. One of the more obscure items on the Masa menu was chawanmushi. It is a steamed custard made with stock and chicken and orange peel and a gingko nut surprise at the bottom of the dish. It inspired me to create this version, which substitutes duck for chicken and foie gras for the gingko nut. Of course, if you don't have foie gras or gingko, feel free to drop in a cashew.

The quality of the chicken stock makes a huge difference in this recipe. Homemade is best.

Ingredients

1⅔ cups (400 mL) duck or chicken stock

3 eggs

Salt and freshly ground black pepper

2 ounces (60 g) duck confit (see recipe page 342), skin removed and meat cut into small cubes

2 ounces (60 g) foie gras, cut into small cubes

1 apple (any kind), peeled, cored and cut into small cubes

2 tablespoons (30 mL) apple cider

1 tablespoon (15 mL) chopped fresh parsley

Directions

Preheat the oven to 300°F (150°C). Heat a kettle of water until hot.

Heat the duck stock in a small saucepan. Whisk the eggs in a medium bowl. While whisking, slowly add the stock to the eggs, a small ladleful at a time. Once half of the stock has been whisked in, pour the rest into this custard mixture and whisk well. Season with salt and pepper.

Place 4 Japanese chawanmushi cups, Chinese tea cups or ceramic ramekins in a baking pan lined with a tea towel. Evenly distribute the duck confit and the foie gras among the cups. Pour the custard mixture into each cup.

Pull the middle rack of the oven out slightly and set the baking pan on it. Carefully pour hot water into the pan until it comes roughly halfway up the sides of the cups. Poach the custards in the oven for approximately 30 minutes or until, when you jiggle the cups, they look and feel set and cohesive and not runny.

Meanwhile, combine the apple pieces and apple cider in a small saucepan. Cover and poach over medium heat for approximately 5 minutes or until the apples are tender and breaking down slightly.

Carefully remove the custard cups from their hot-water bath and set each cup on a small plate. Spoon a small amount of cooked apple on top of each custard (you may not use all the apple). Sprinkle with chopped parsley and serve.

Bolognese Sauce

Makes 6 servings

It is interesting how some home-cooked dishes become important reminders of childhood and growing up. It is as though the recipe is only part of the experience. Nourishment of another sort is derived from the comfort of having a family member prepare the dish in familiar surroundings with the gang all present. Such is the case with this Kennedy family classic.

Ingredients

¼ cup (60 mL) fine olive oil

2 pounds (1 kg) ground beef

3 medium onions, finely chopped

5 cloves garlic, finely minced

2 carrots, diced

2 celery stalks, diced

2 bay leaves

1 tablespoon (15 mL) dried oregano

Freshly ground black pepper

½ cup (125 mL) red wine

8 cups (2 L) J.K. Tomato Sauce (see recipe page 133)

Salt

Directions

Place a large pot over medium heat. Add the olive oil and the ground beef. Cook for about 20 minutes, stirring regularly. When most of the liquid has evaporated, add the onions, garlic, carrots, celery and bay leaves. Continue to cook, stirring, for 10 minutes. Add the oregano and black pepper to taste and continue to stir. When the vegetables begin to brown, add the red wine. Keep stirring. When the red wine has evaporated, add the tomato sauce. Continue to cook until the sauce is the desired consistency. Season with salt and discard the bay leaves. Serve over spaghetti with finely grated Parmigiano-Reggiano or, as pictured here, over fries, as mini poutine.

Acknowledgements

I would like to acknowledge and thank my co-authors, Ivy and Jo; my staff at Jamie Kennedy Kitchens; the team at HarperCollins; and the people who are the inspiration for this book—the local food community.

—JAMIE

I am very thankful to Jamie for giving me the opportunity to work on my very first book, and to Jo for being such a wonderful collaborator and photographer. Thanks to everyone at HarperCollins—Rob Firing, Kirsten Hanson and Noelle Zitzer especially. Biggest thanks of all to my husband, Kerry Knight, for taking on the daunting task of formatting every one of these recipes.

—IVY

Thank you, Jamie! It's been an honour and a privilege to document you and your work. You've been so cooperative and supportive since the very first day I took your photo back in 2007. Thank you, Ivy, for bringing the project to life, and to Kirsten Hanson and everyone at HarperCollins. Thank you to my family and friends for all their support, especially to my mother who taught me how to hold a camera properly and to print in the darkroom, and to both my parents for their unconditional love and encouragement.

—JO

At left and throughout the book are elements from Tom Dean's installation work *Fire and Sausage: Small Mercies*, commissioned by the City of Toronto for Nuit Blanche, 2009.

Index

C

385

Z

Jamie
KENNEDY
Kitchens